ZenArt Editions

Harmonious Gardens

Relaxing Coloring Book

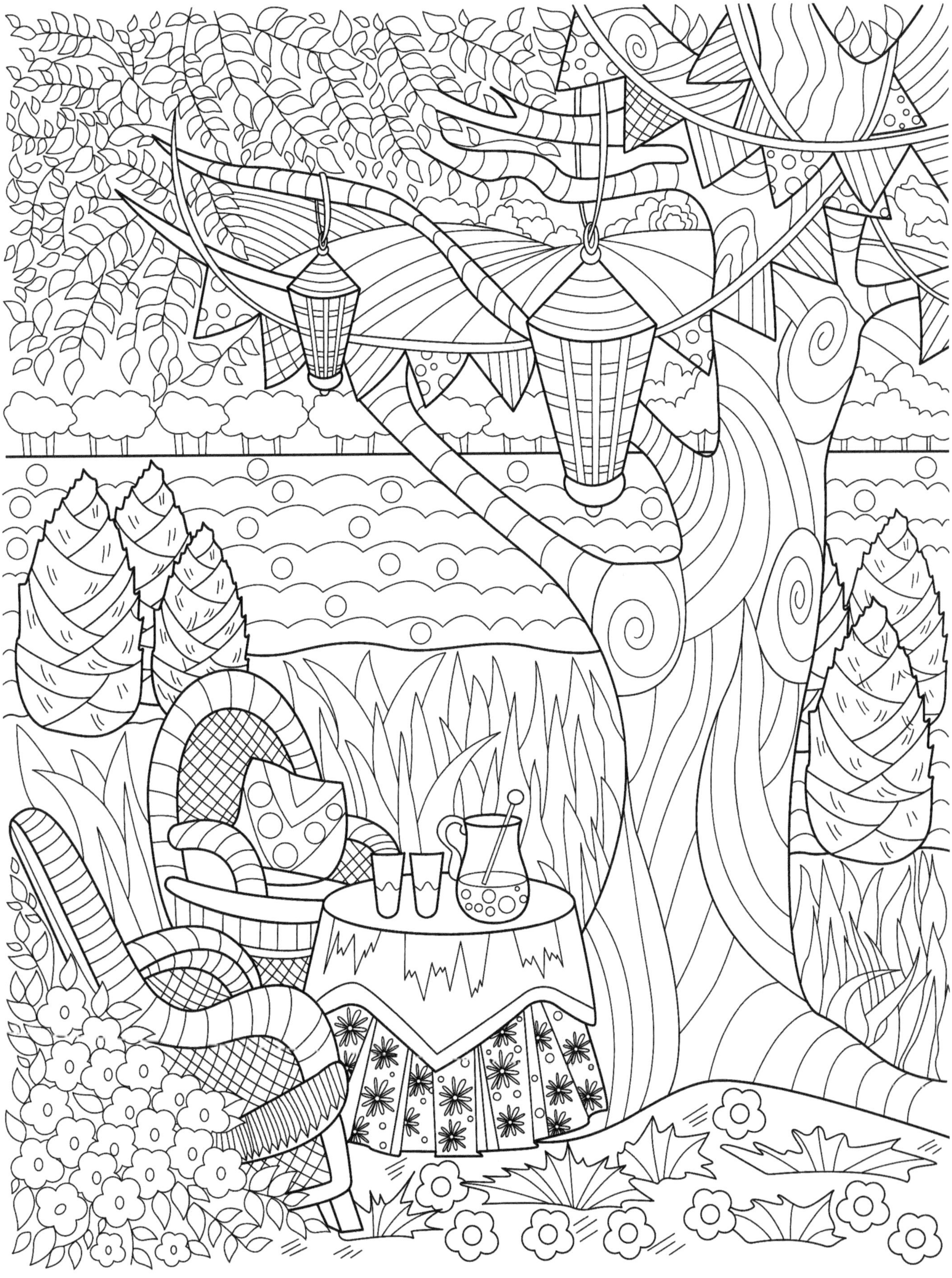

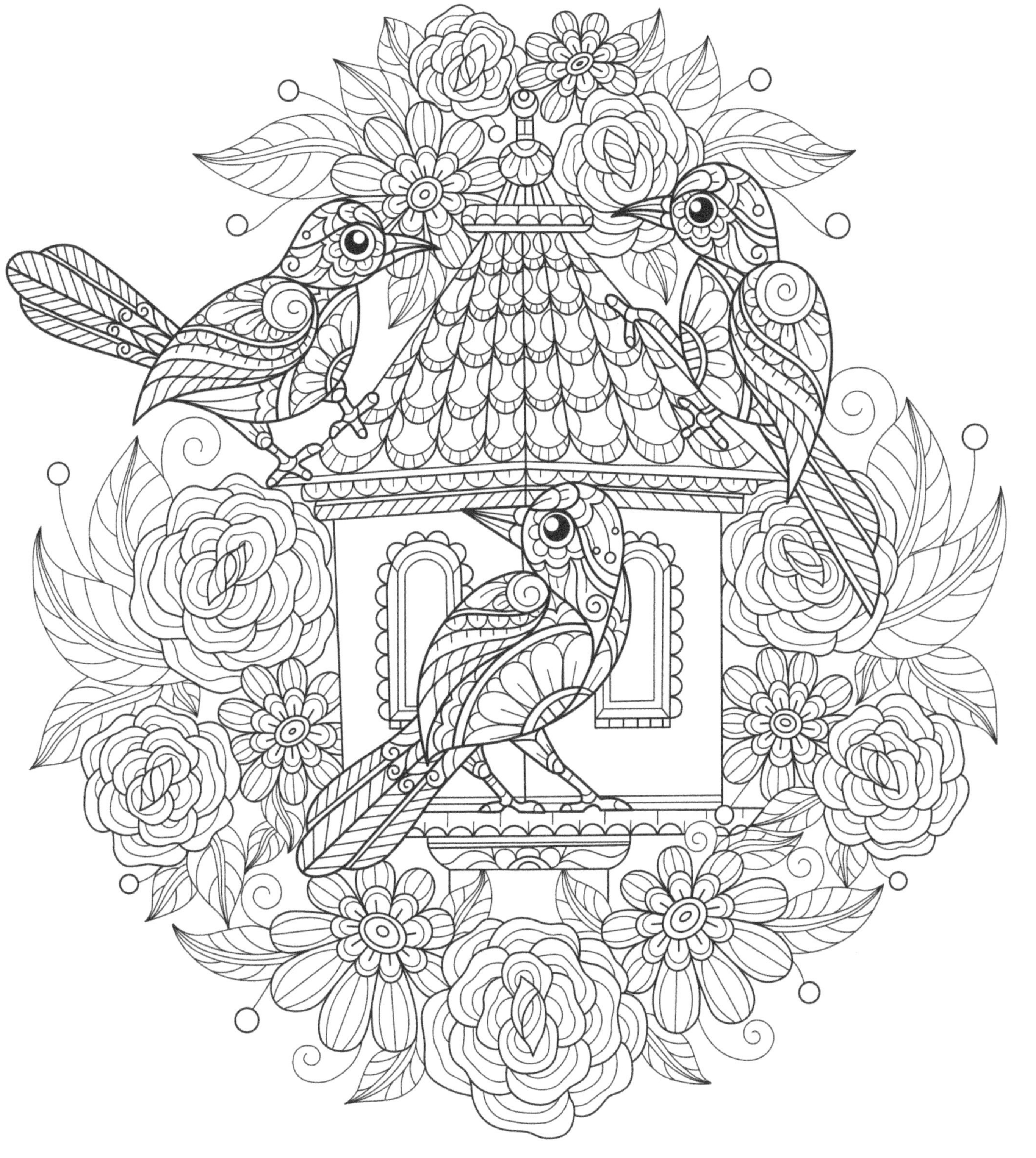

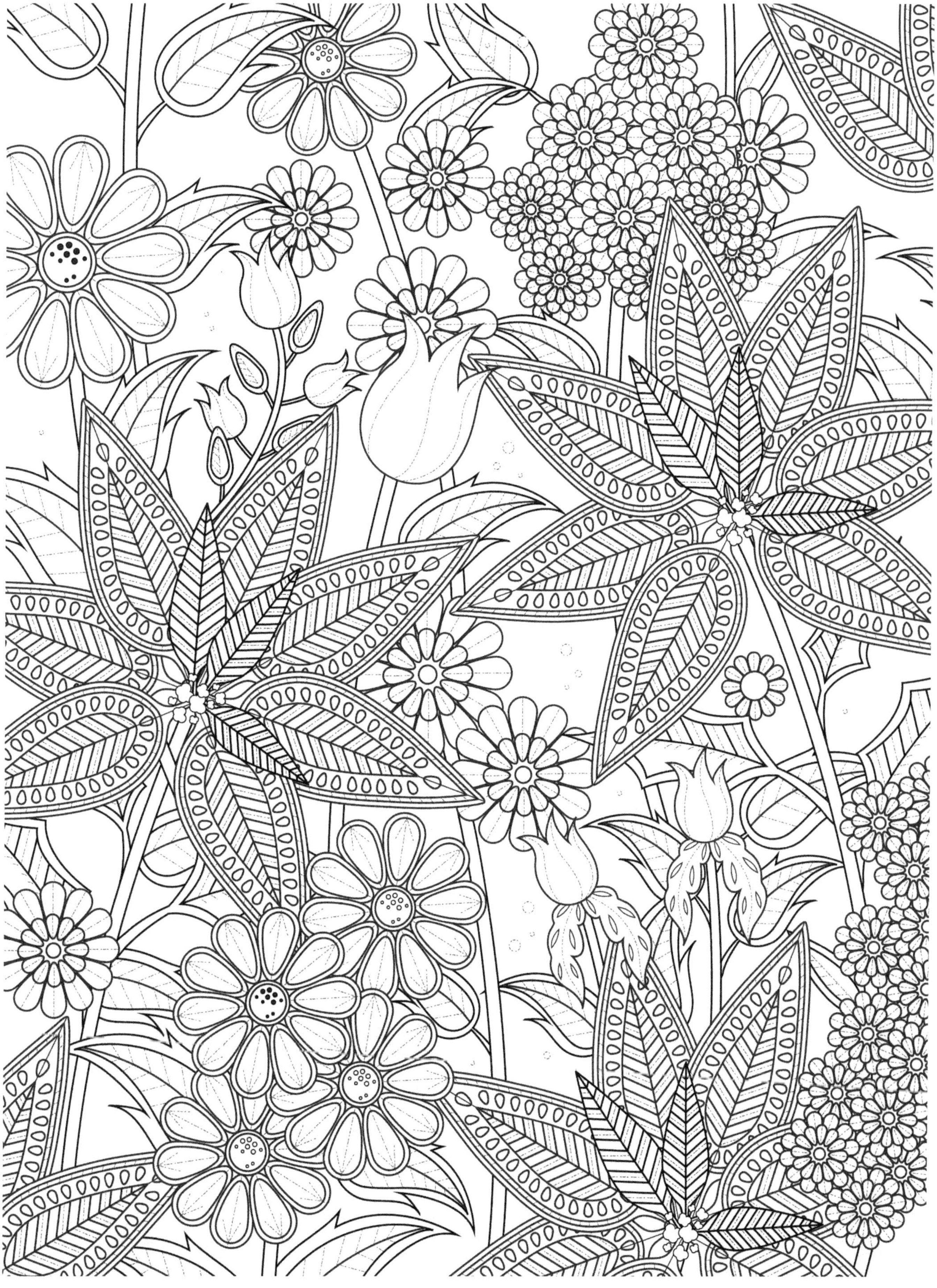

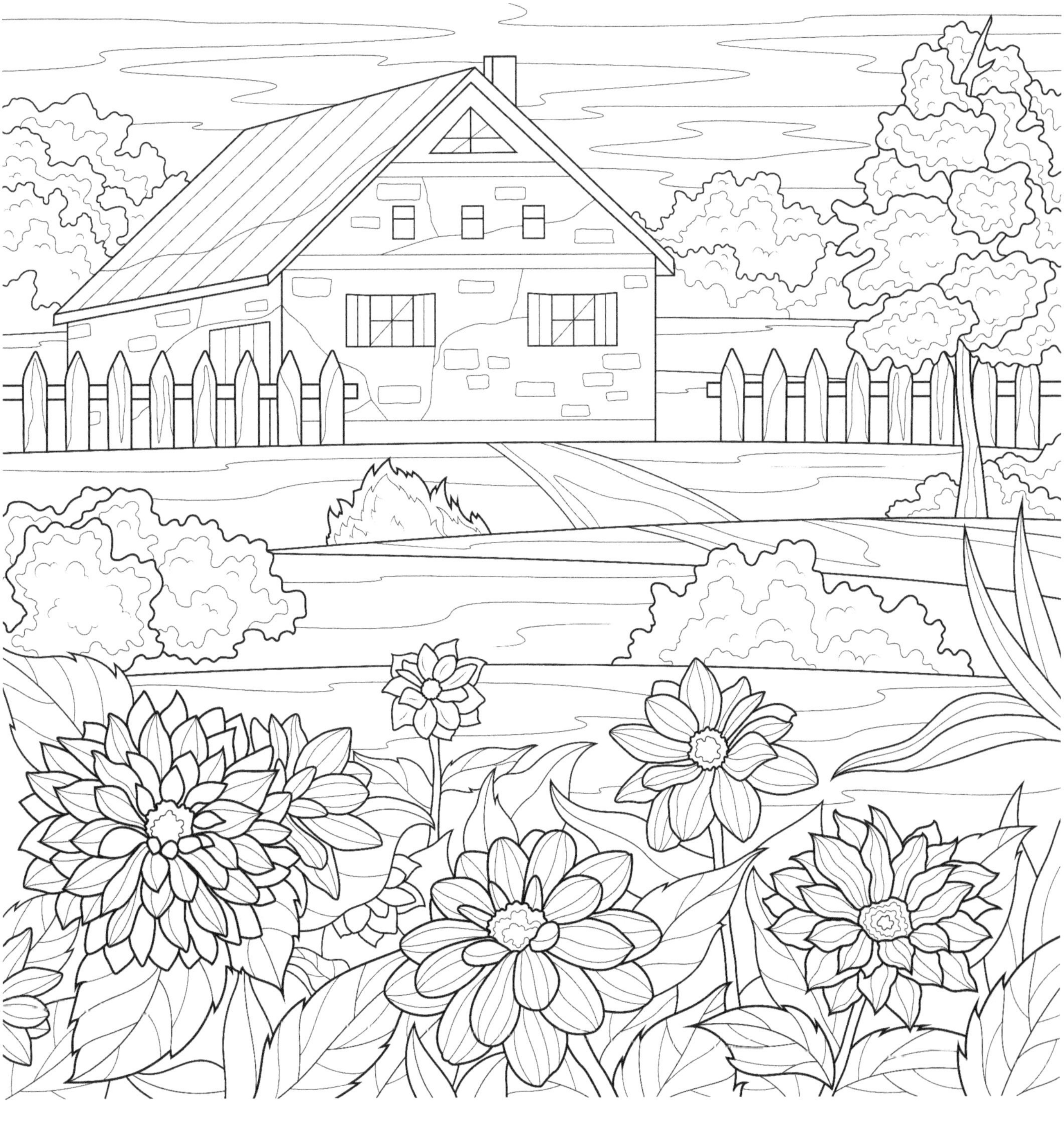

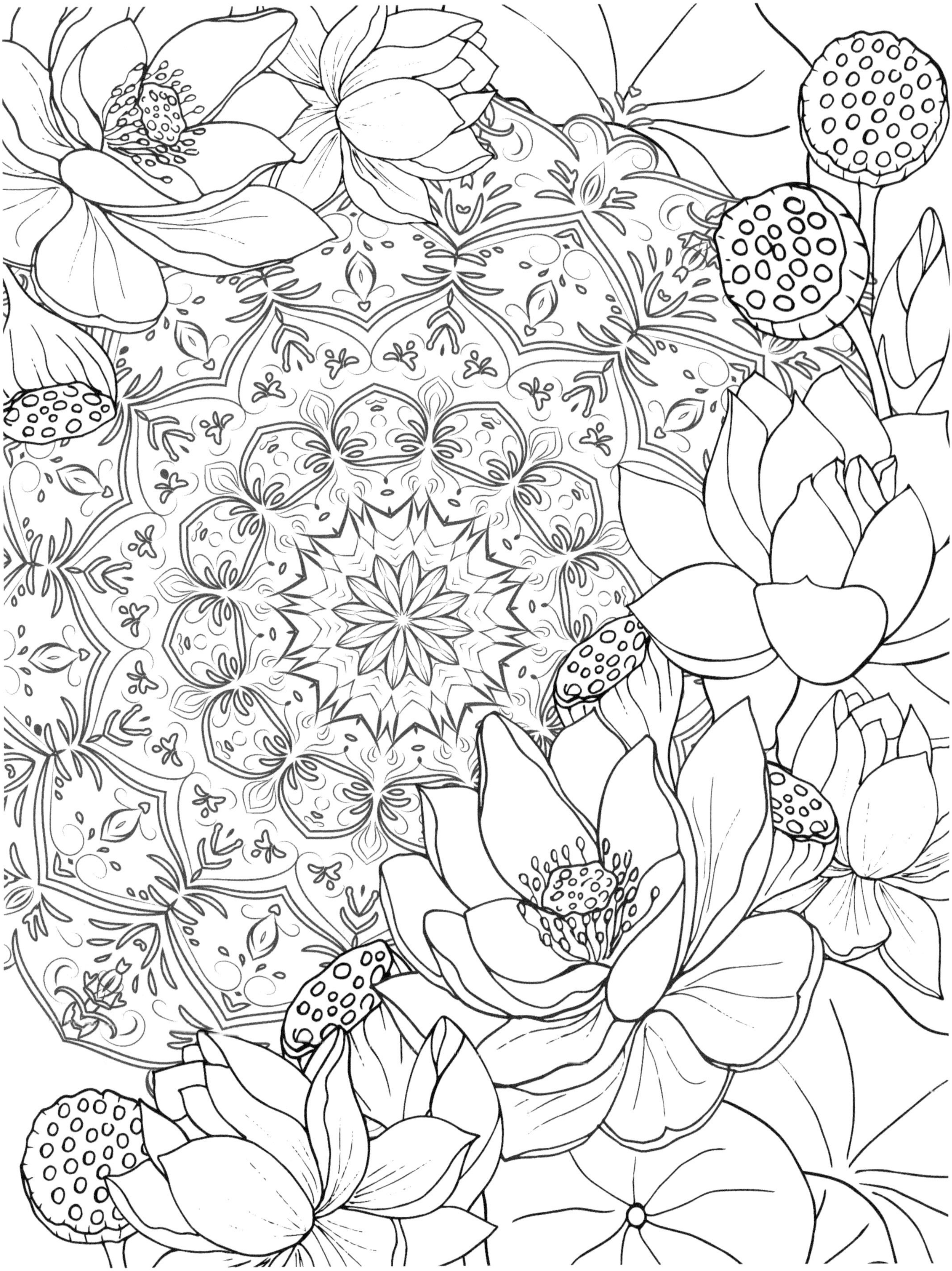

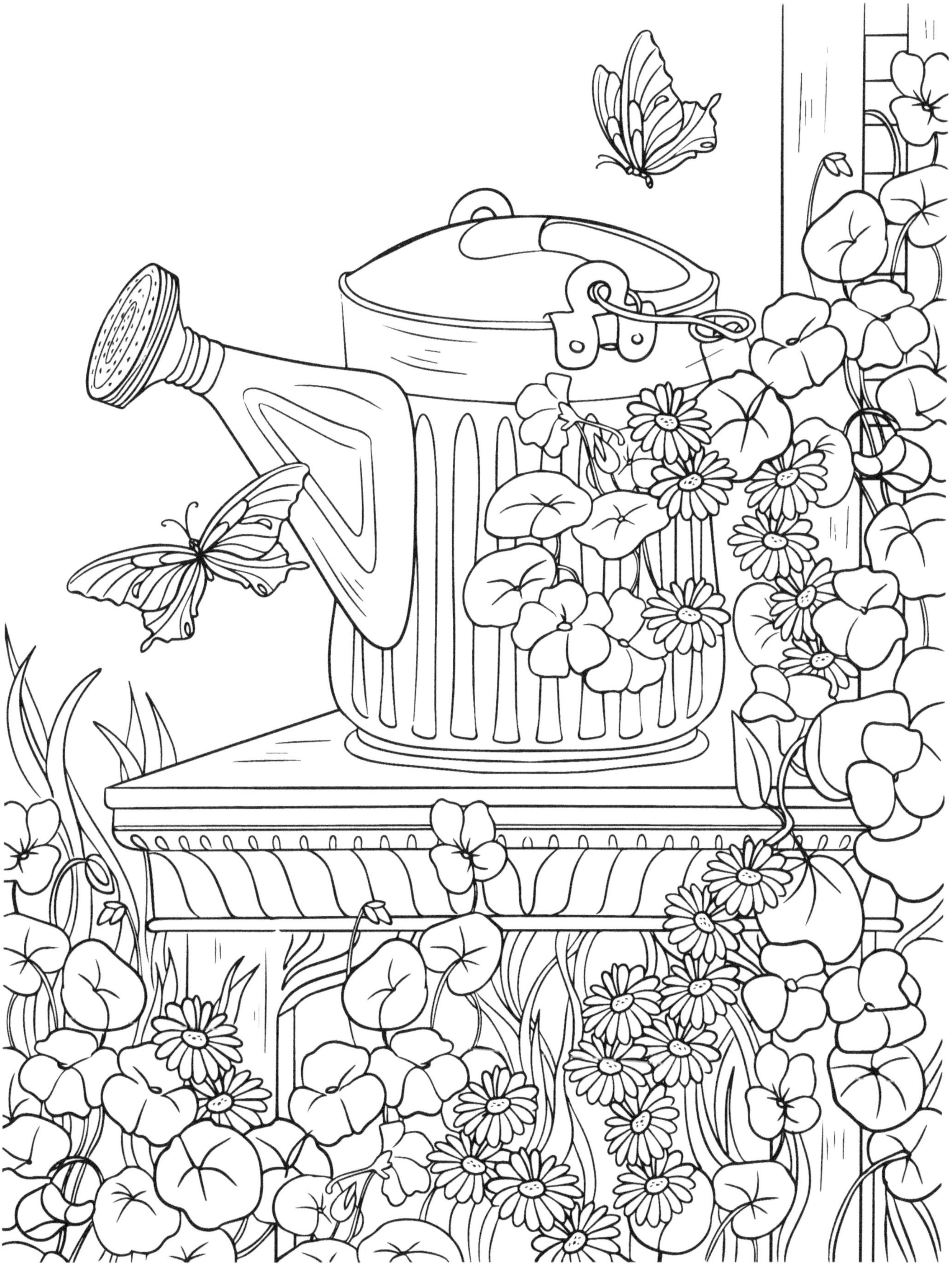

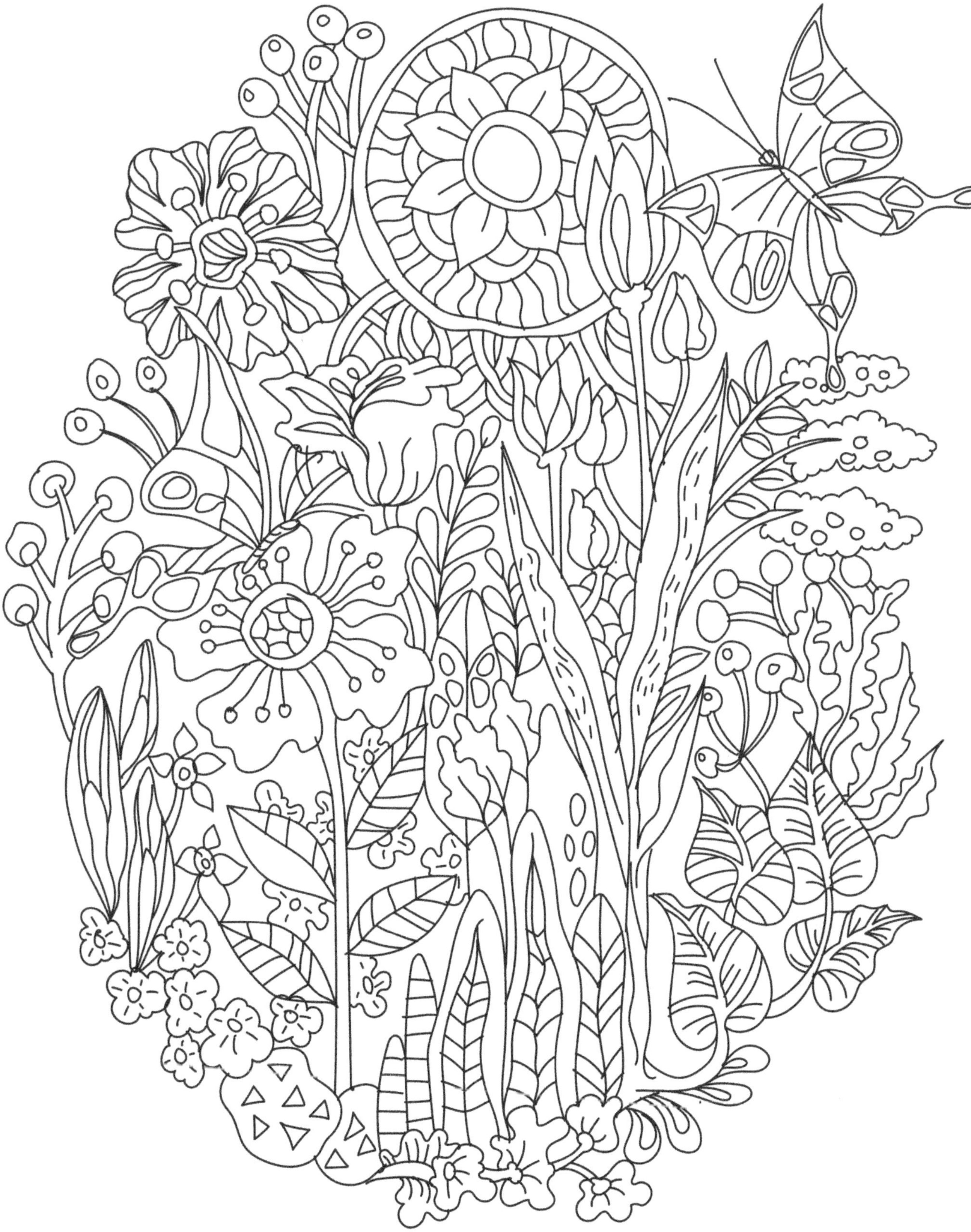

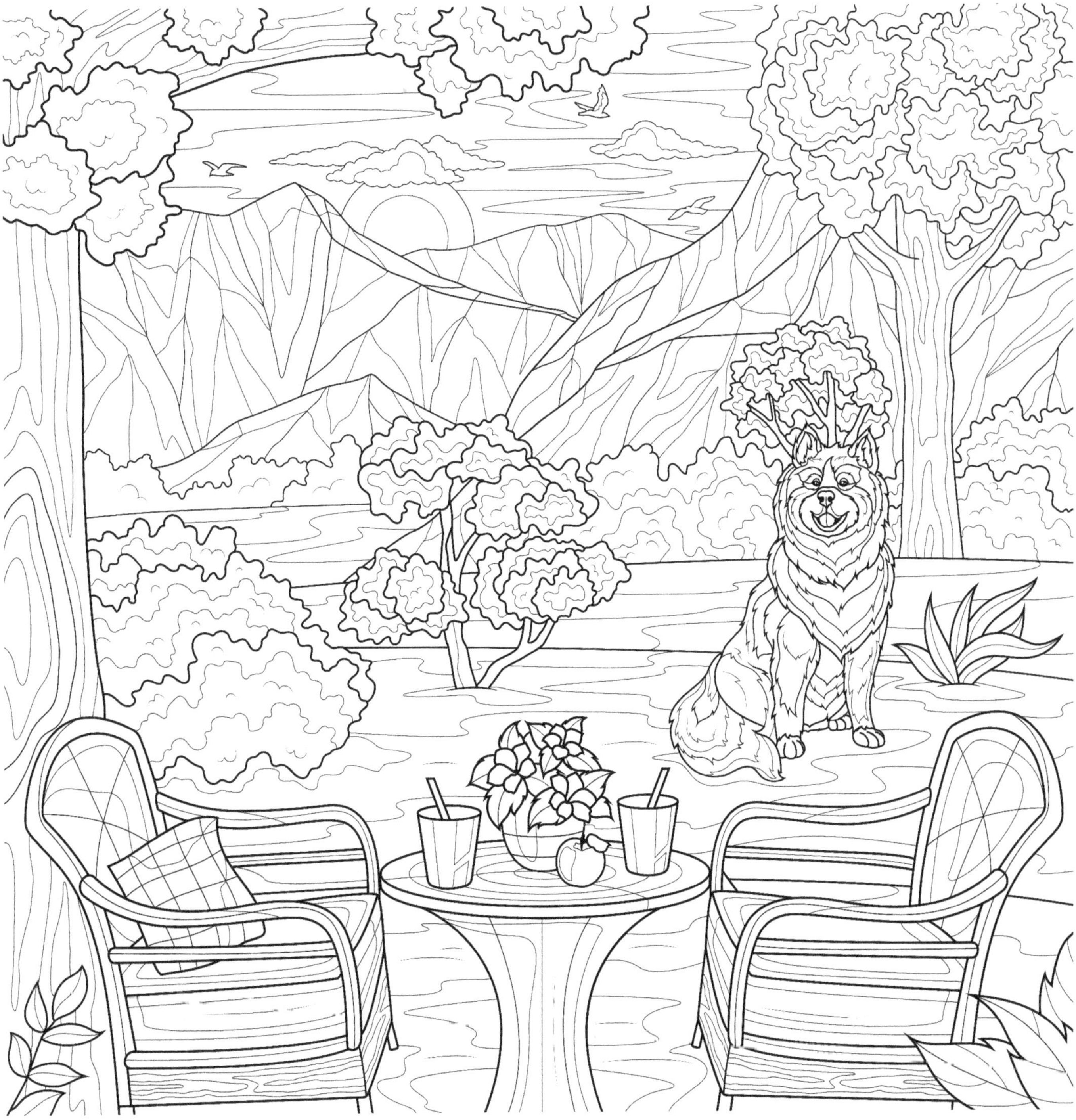

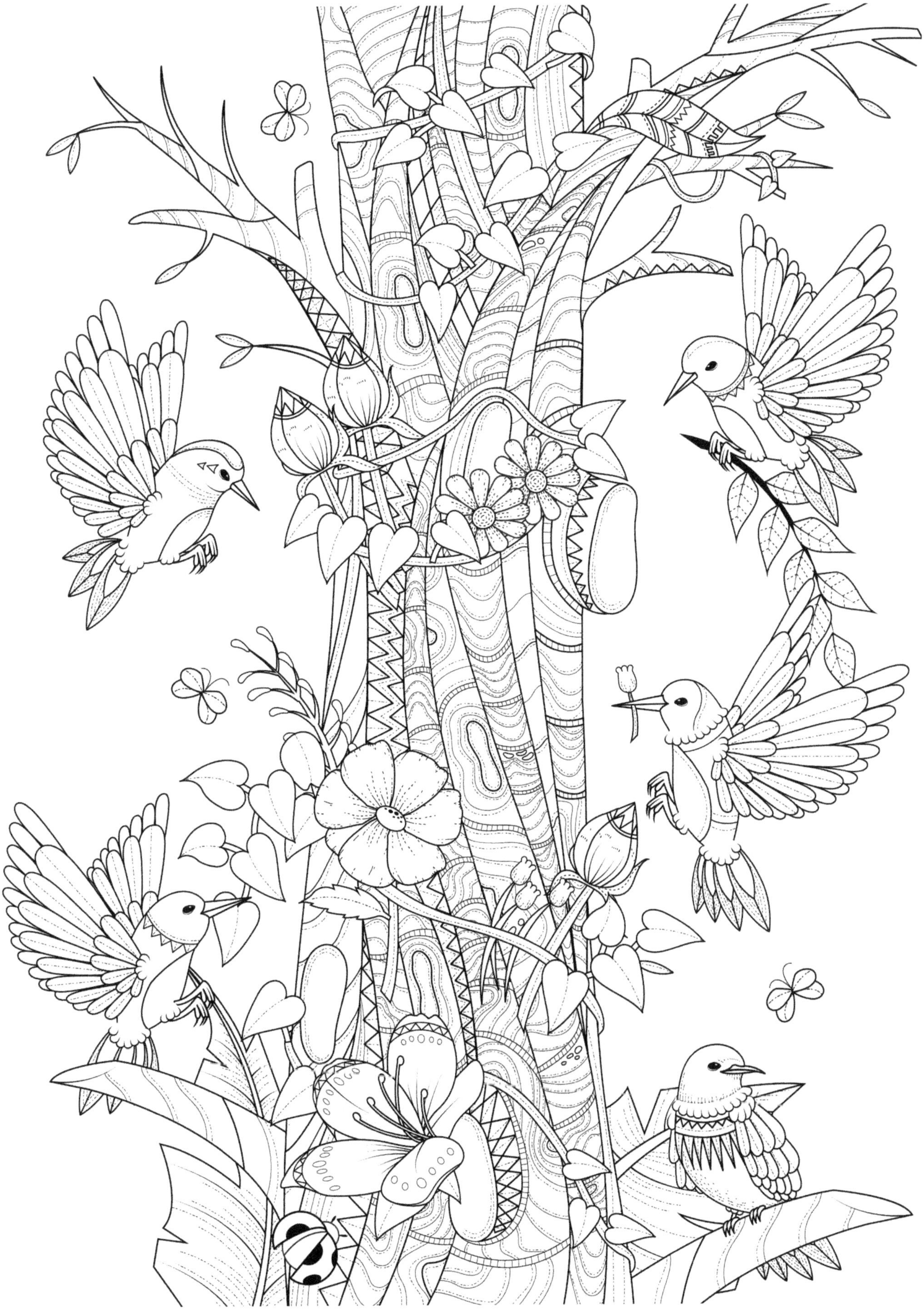

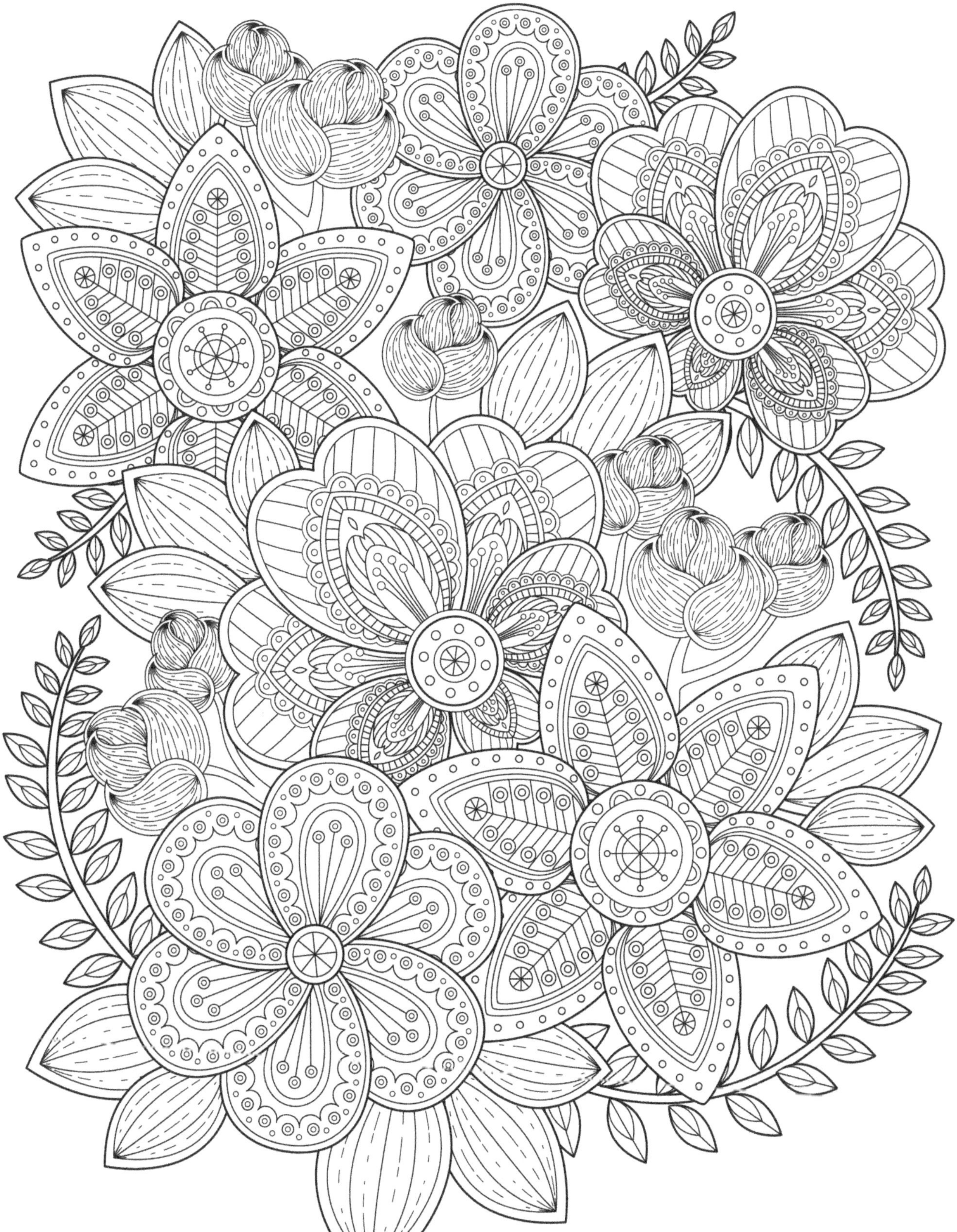

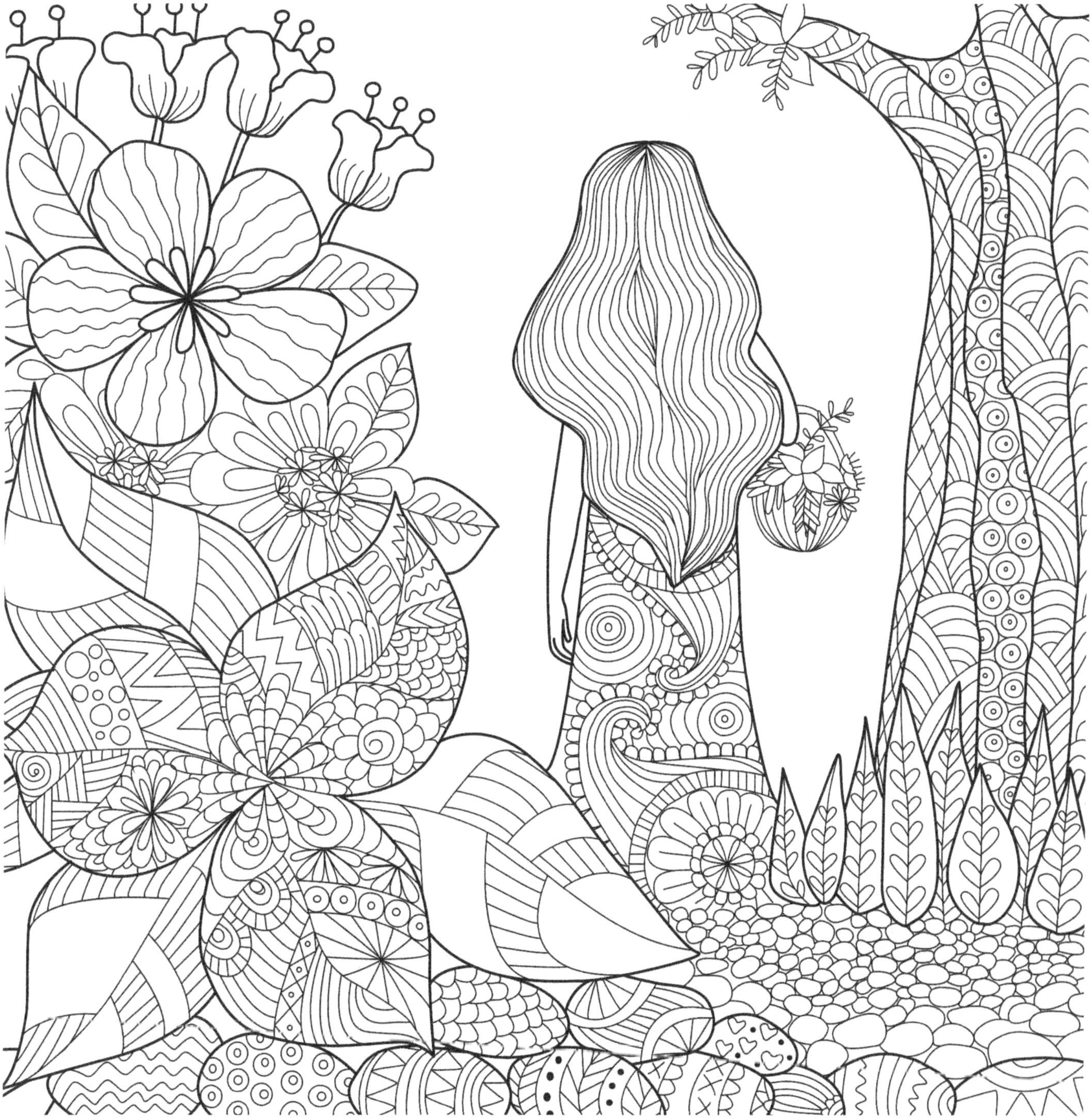

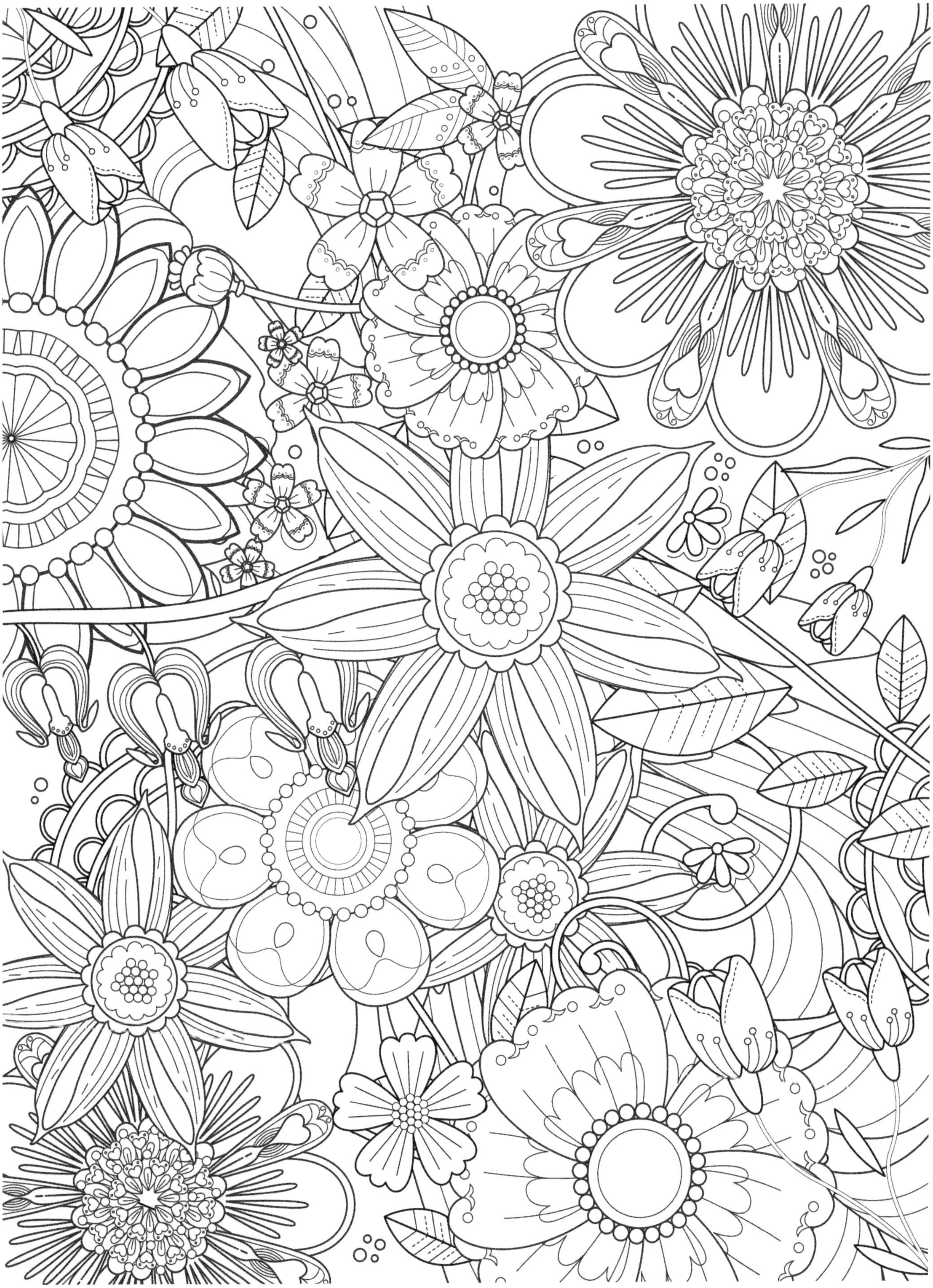

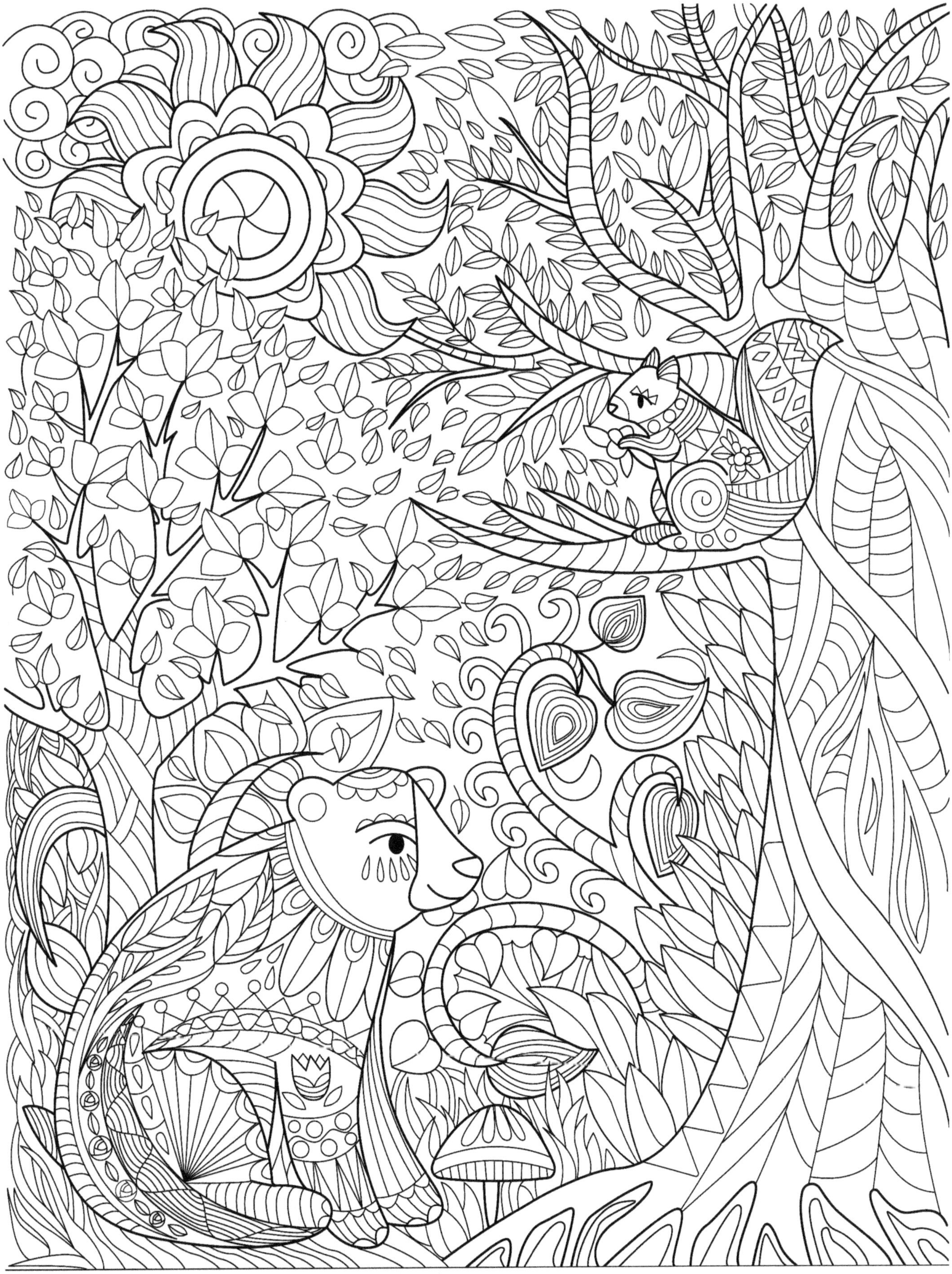

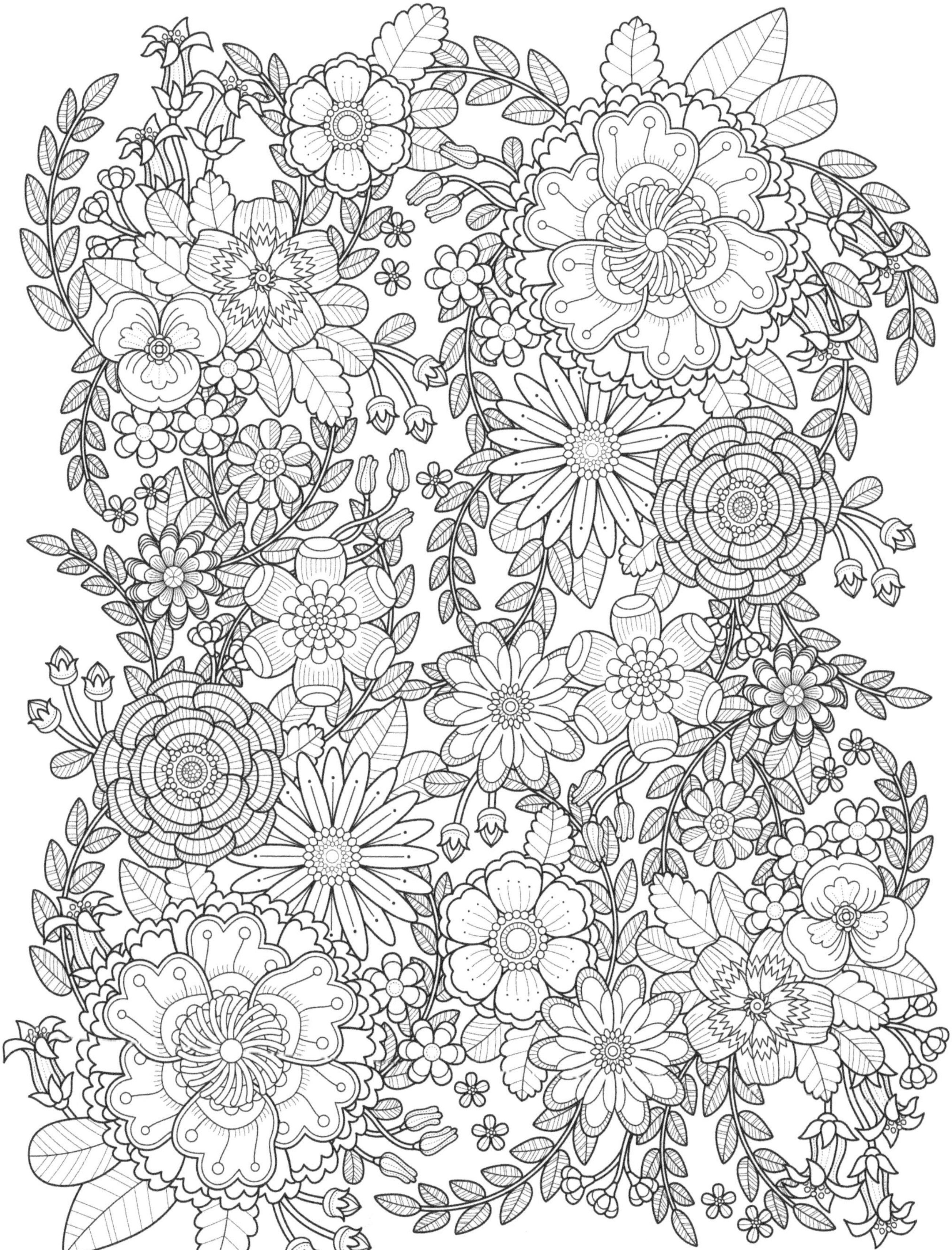

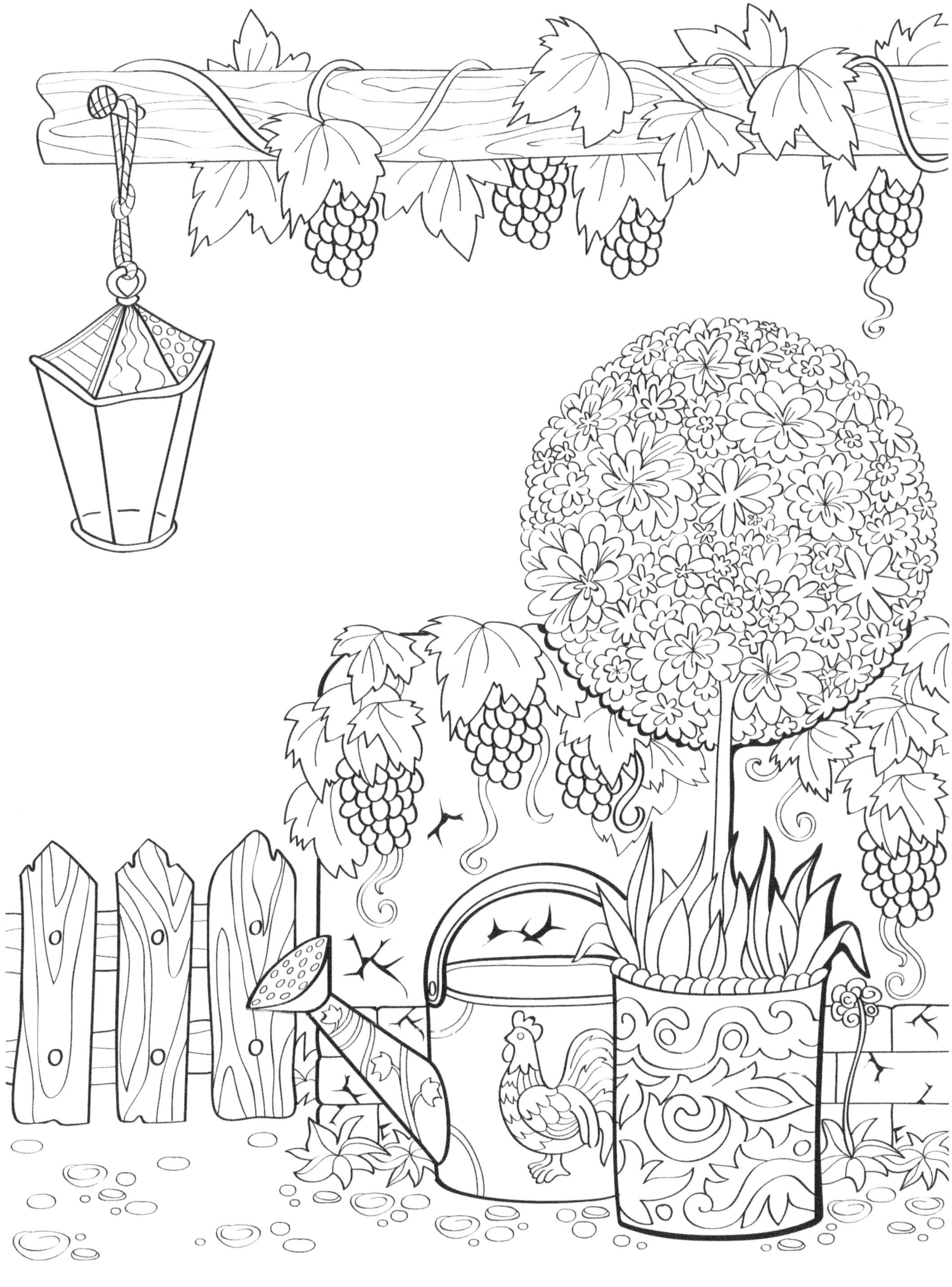

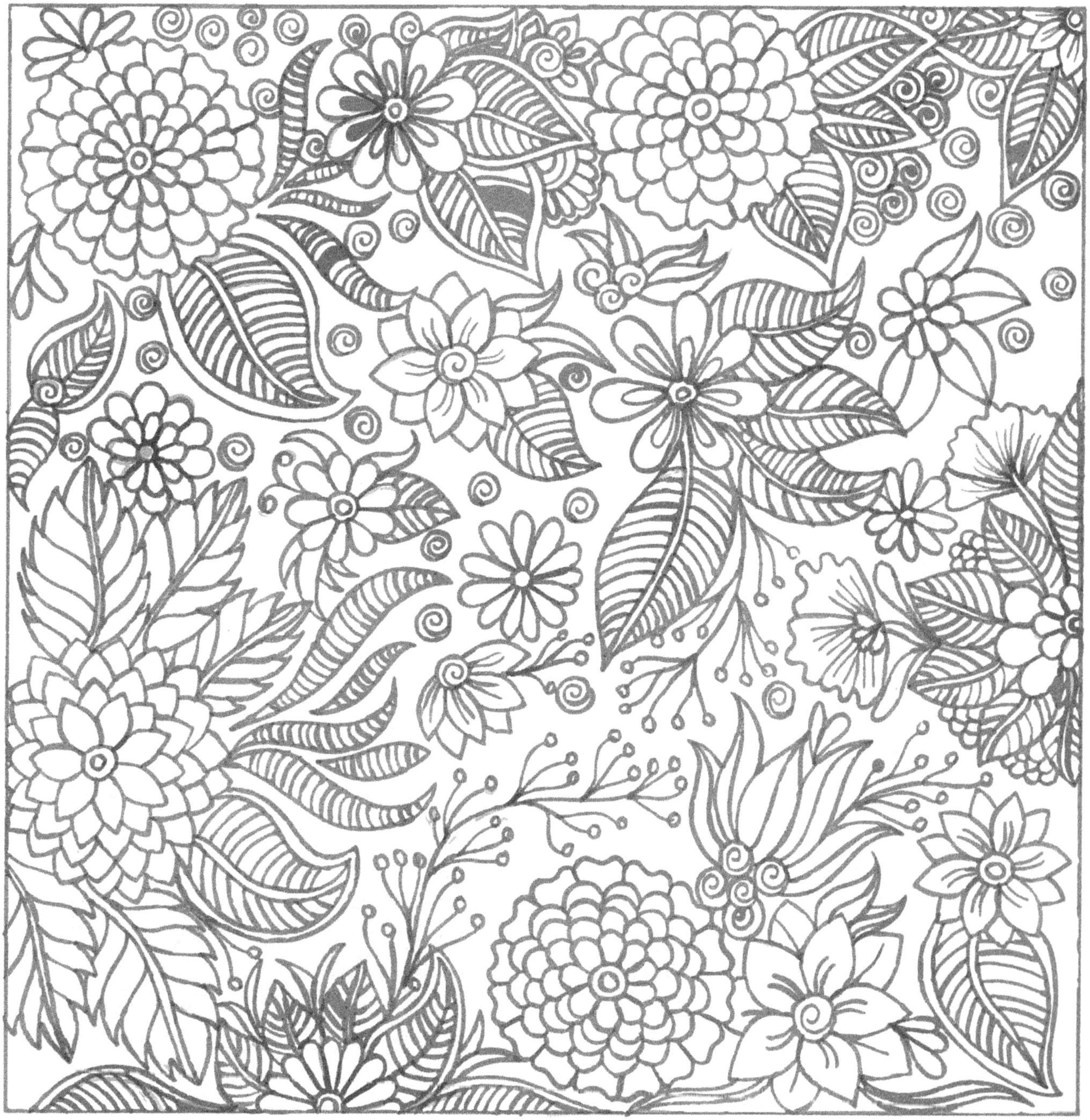

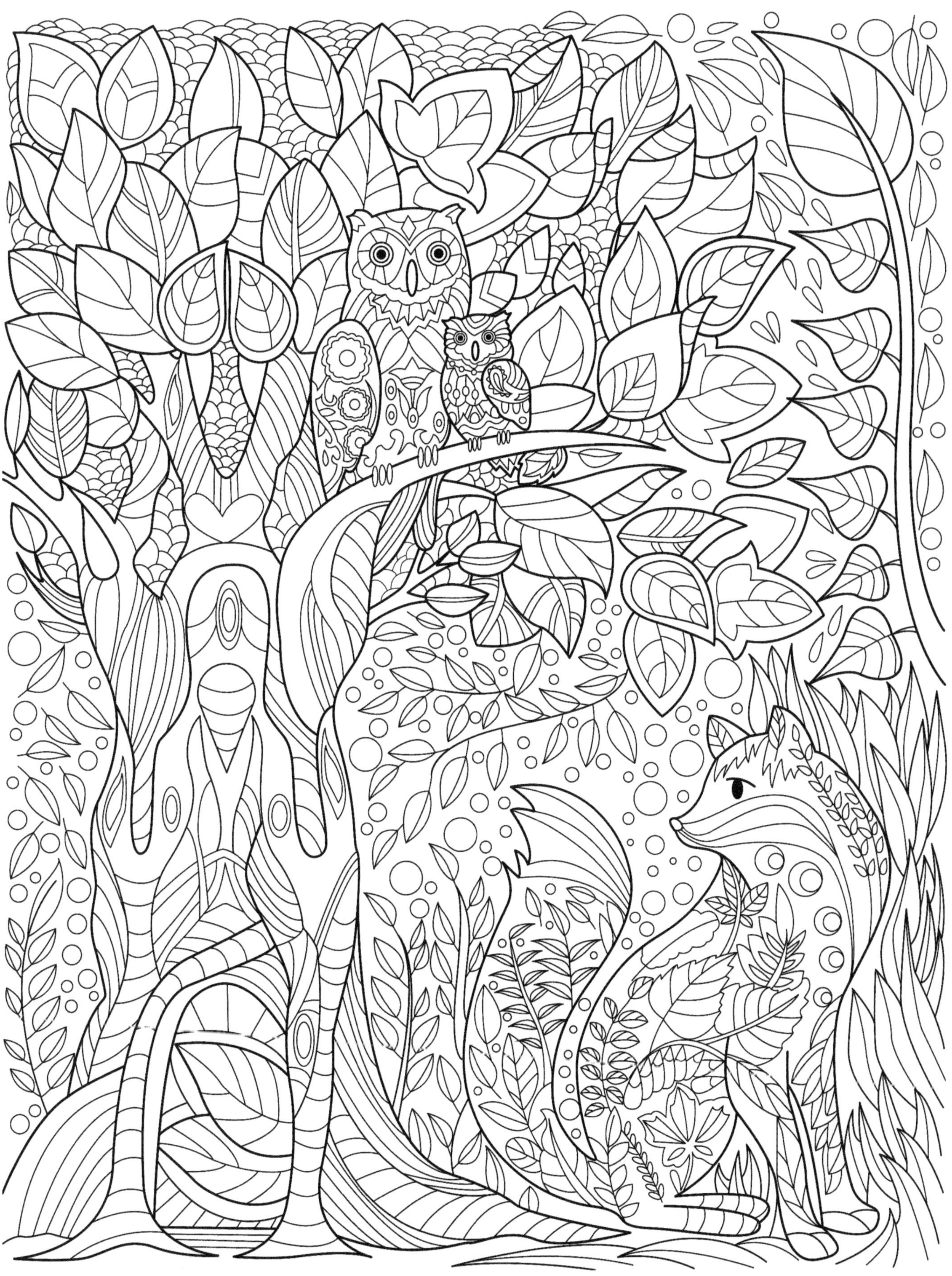

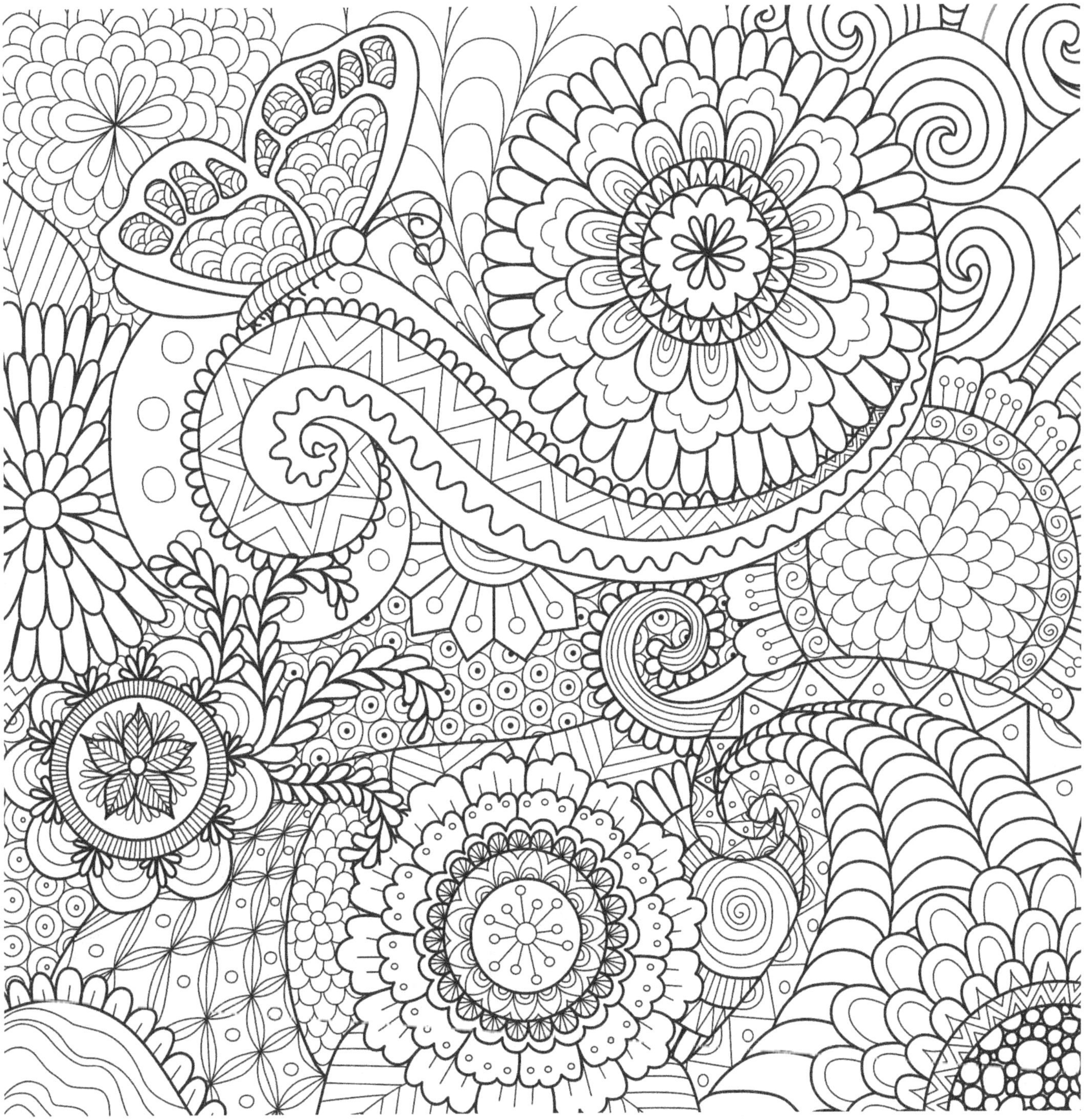

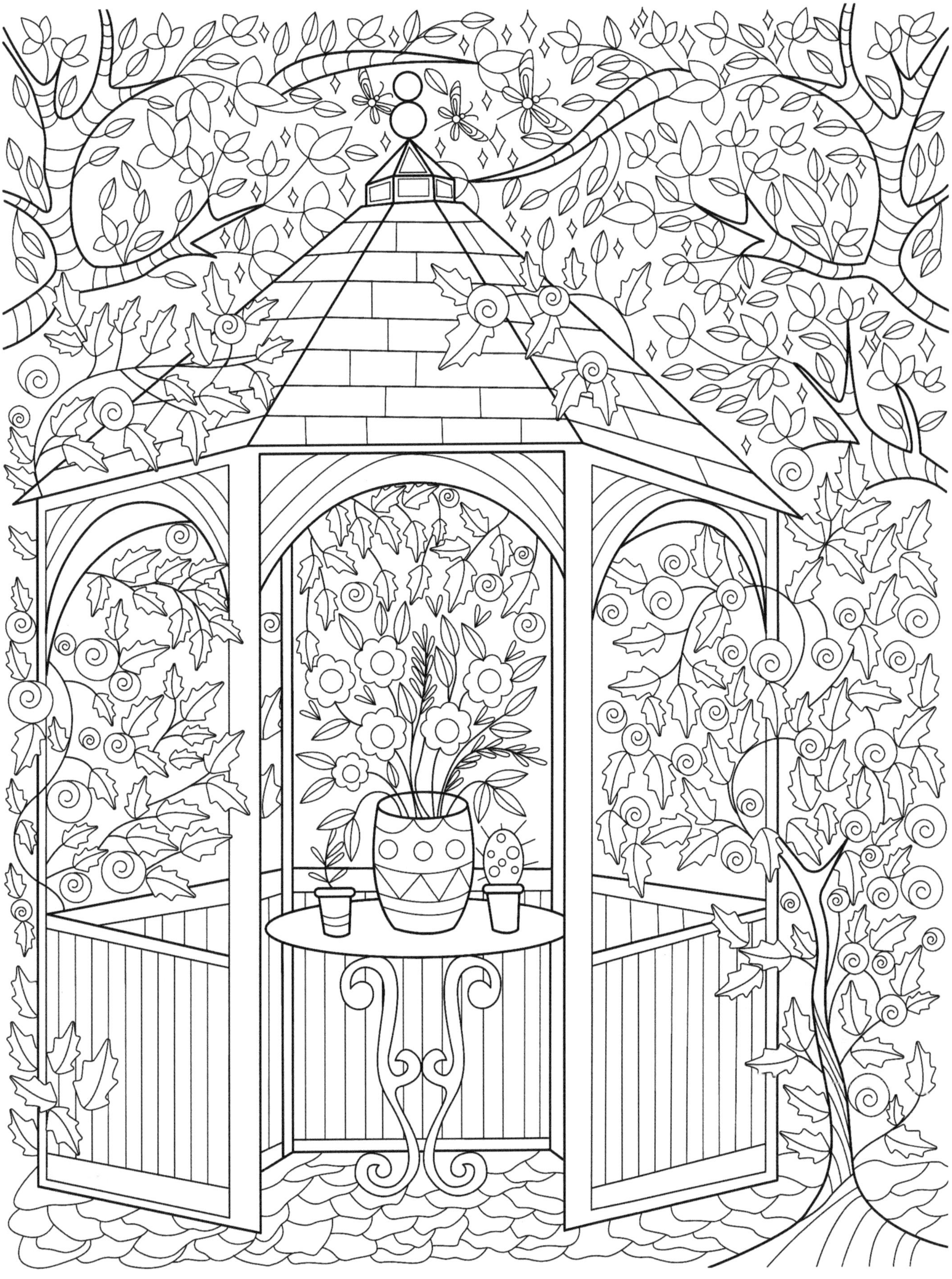

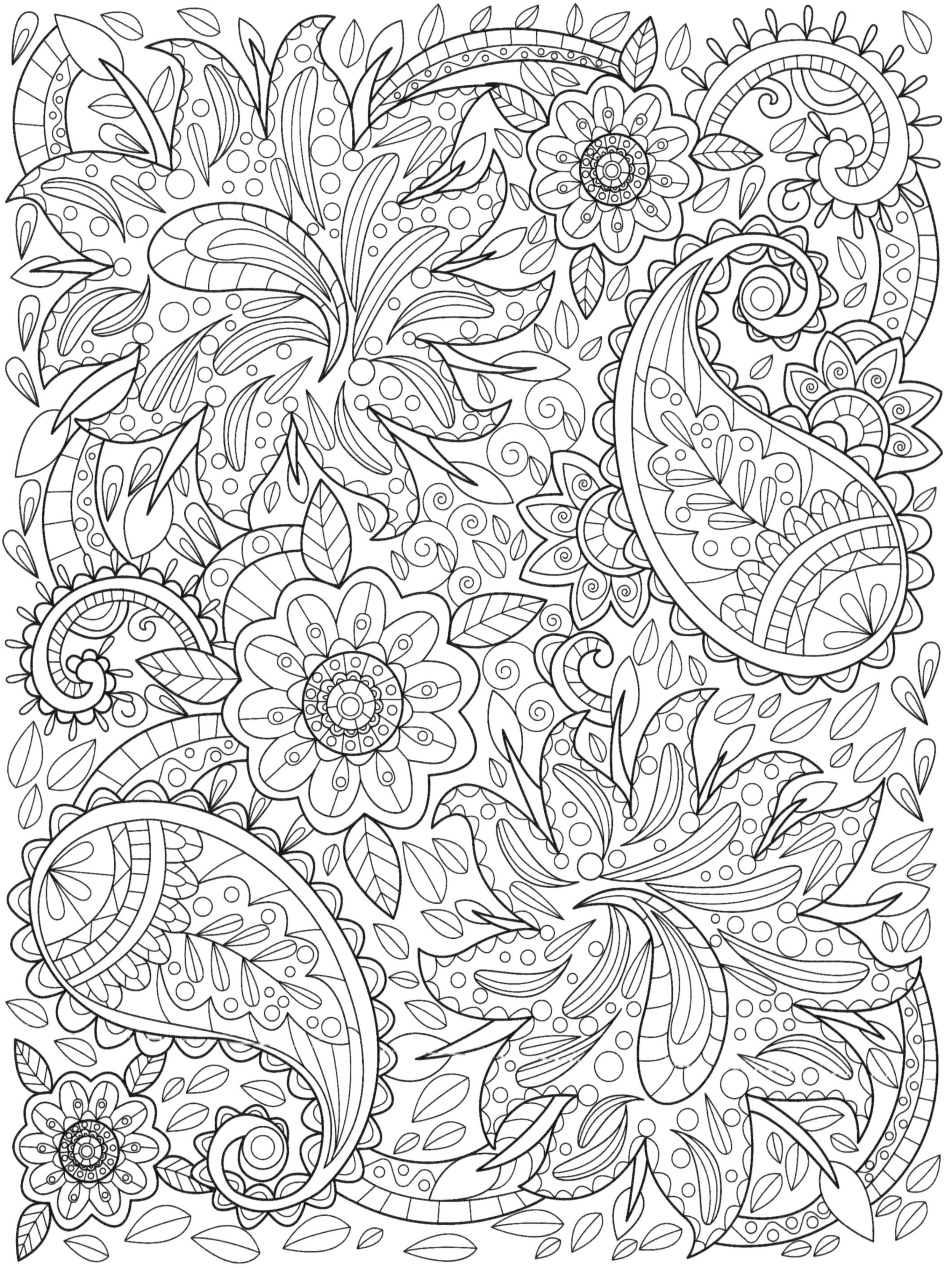

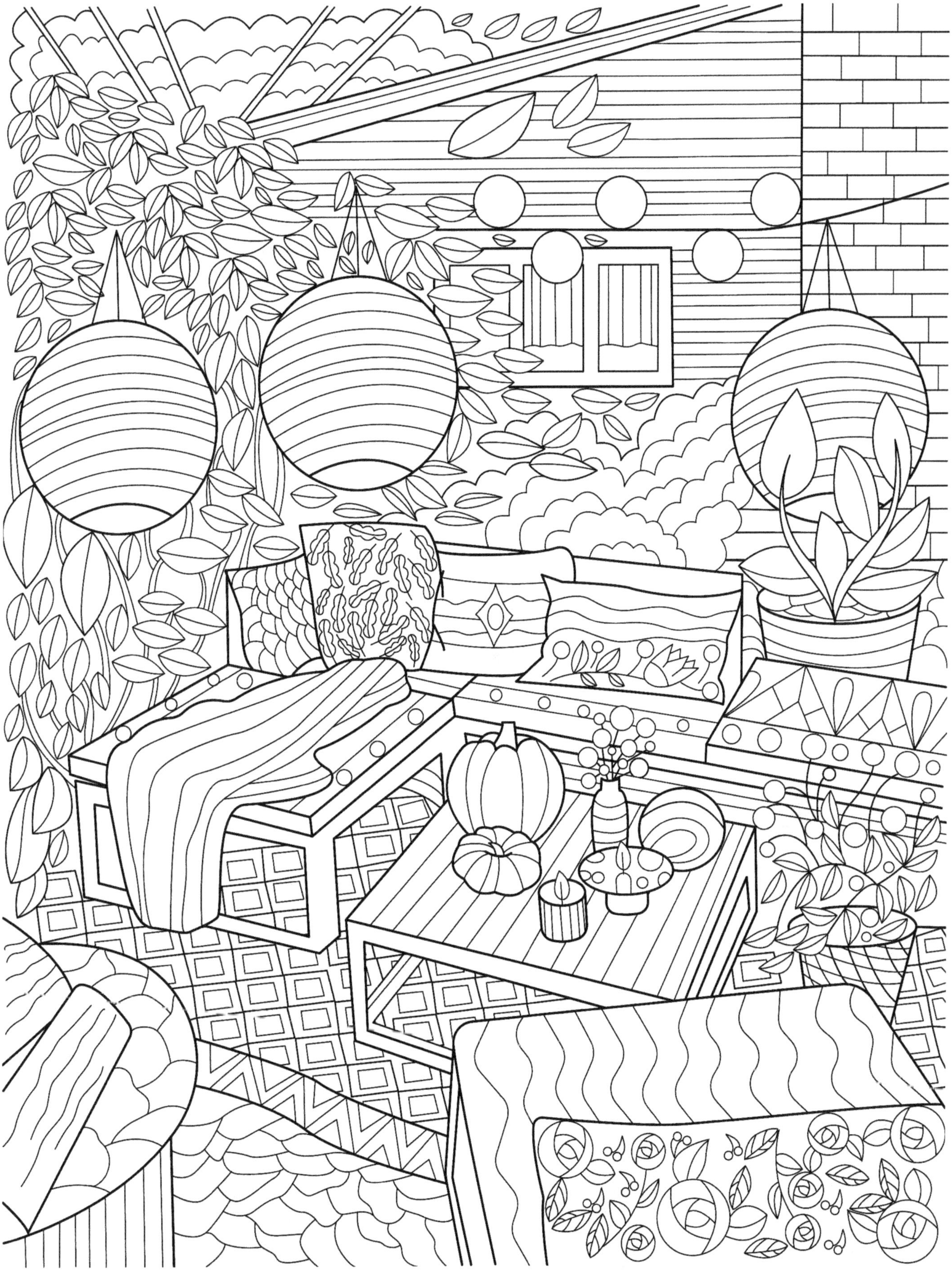

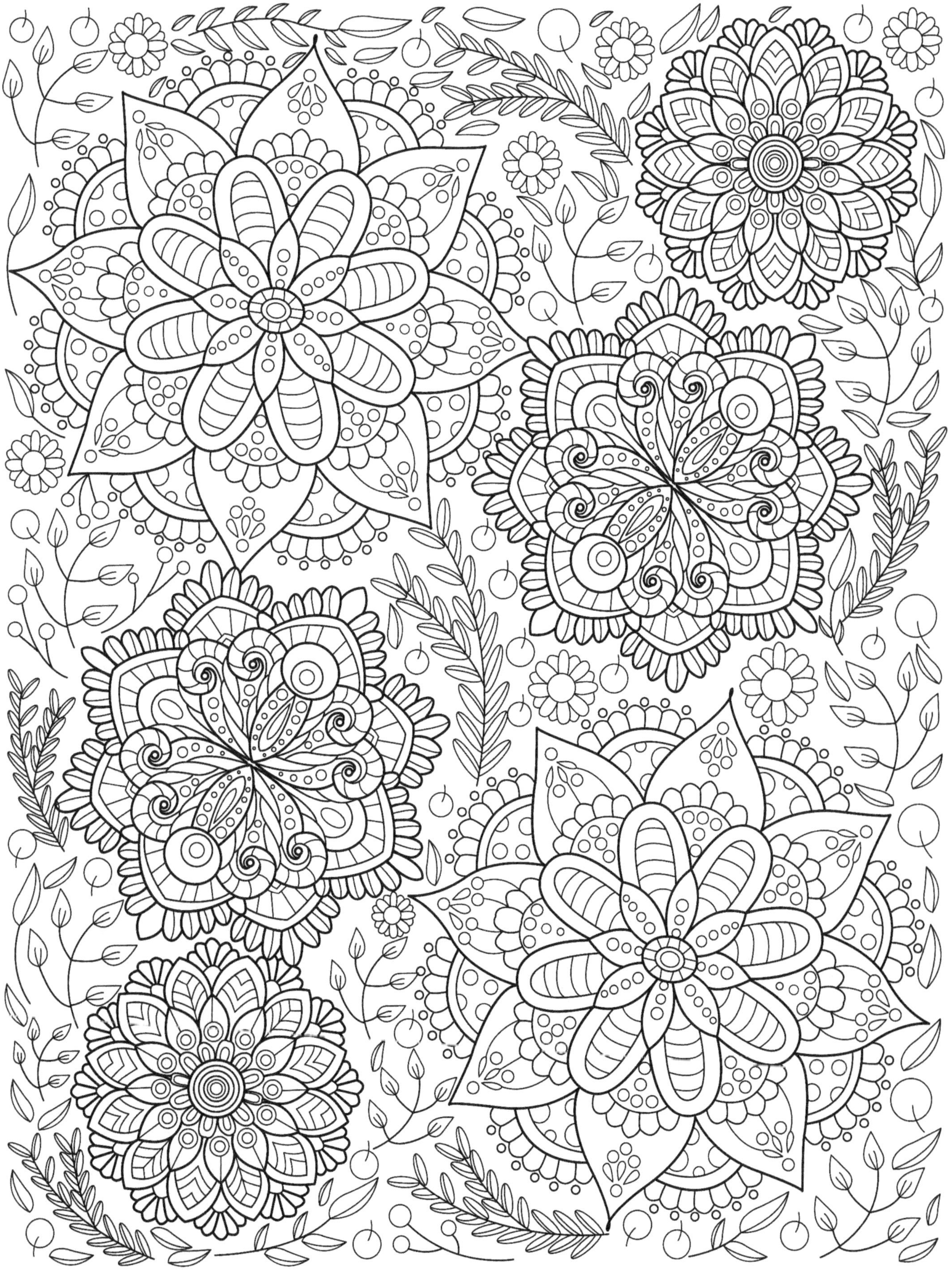

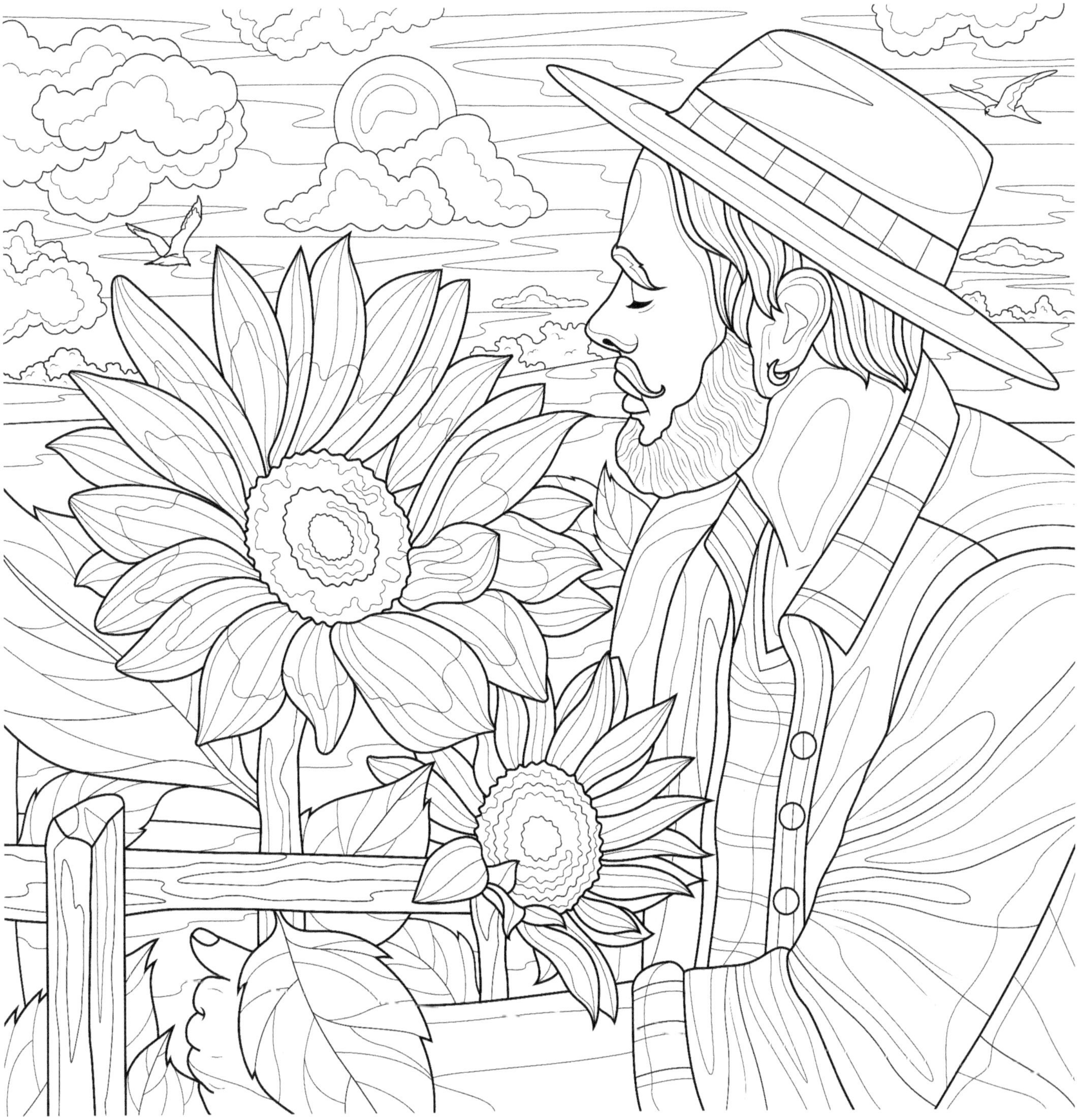

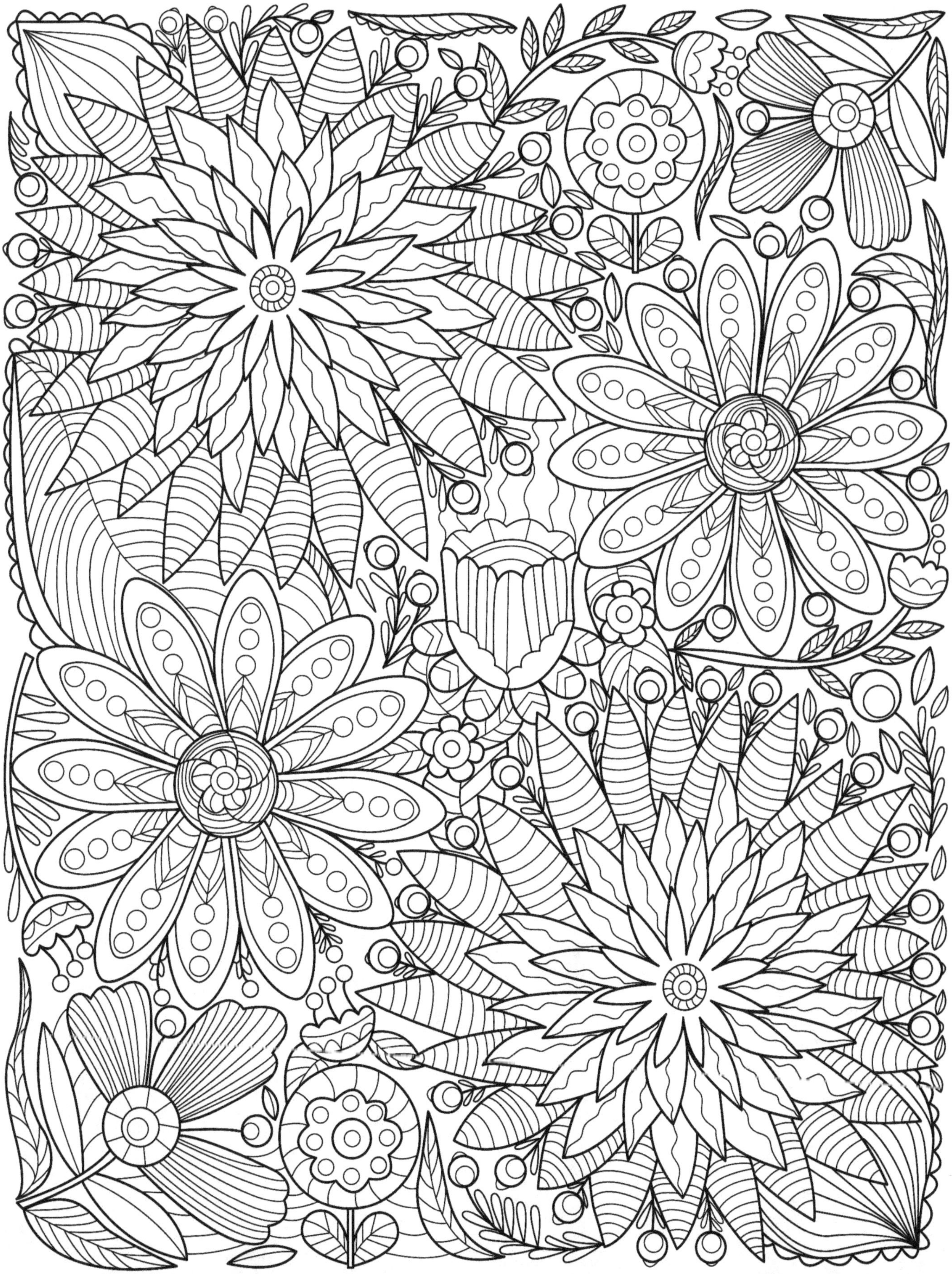

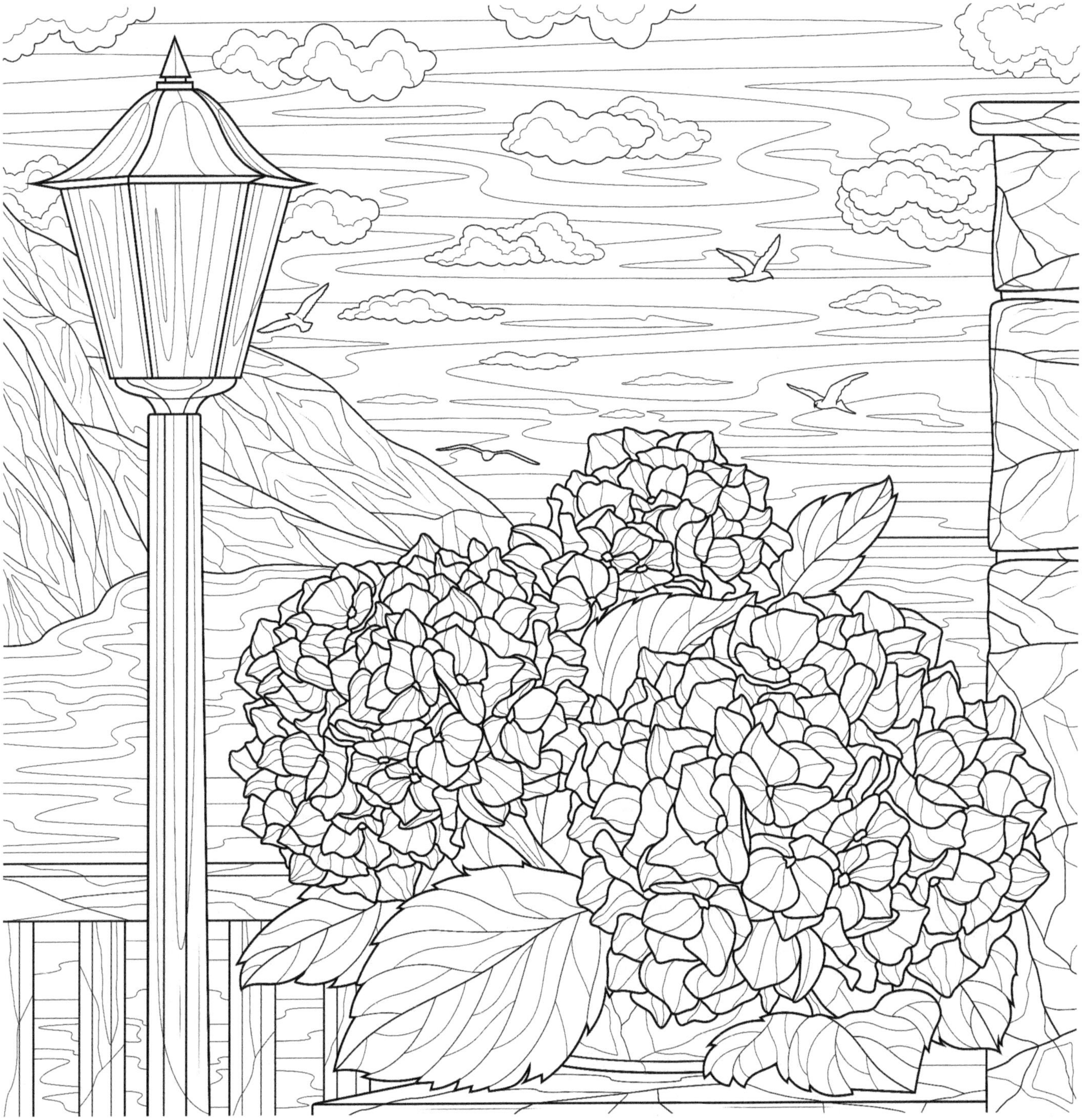

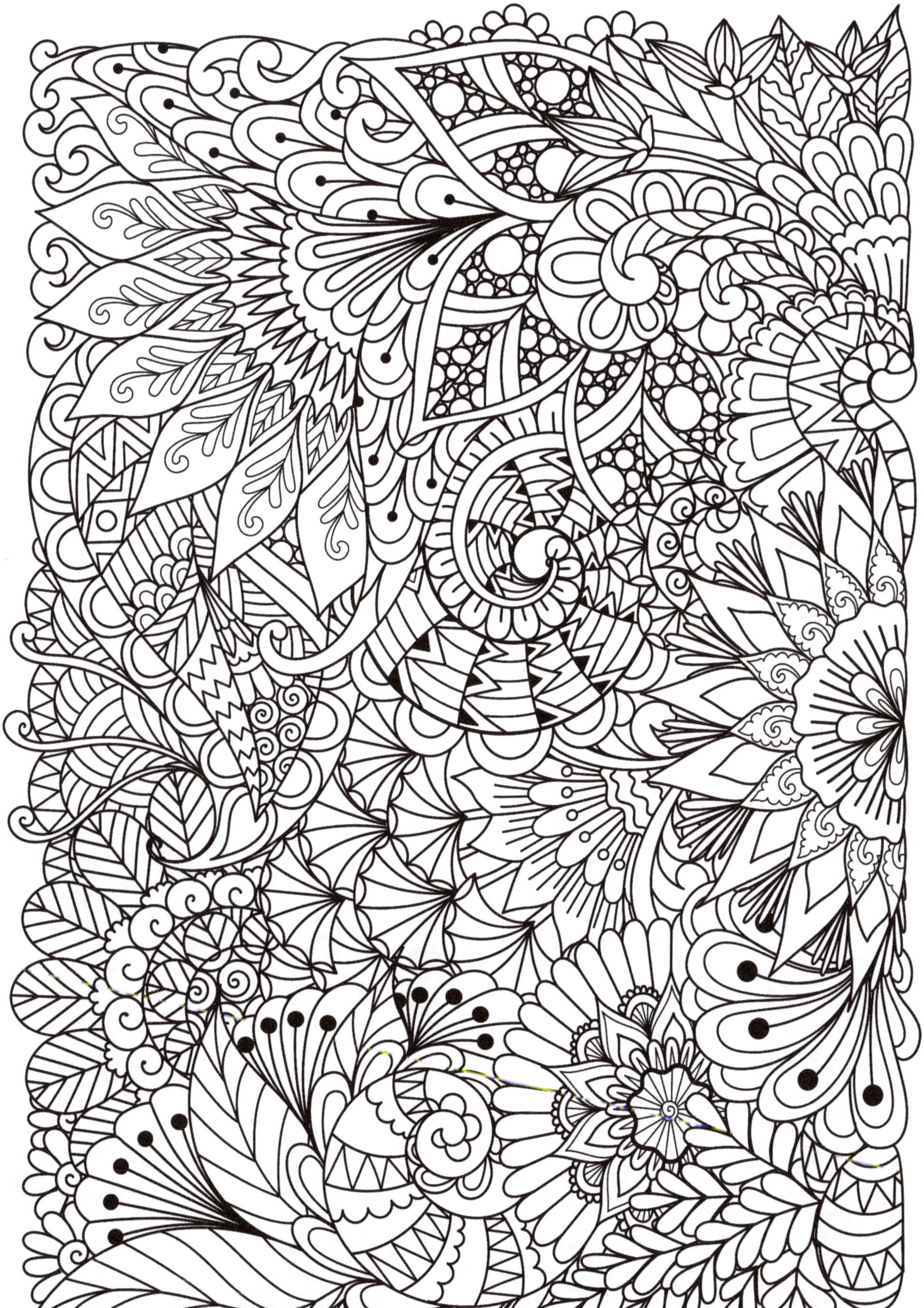

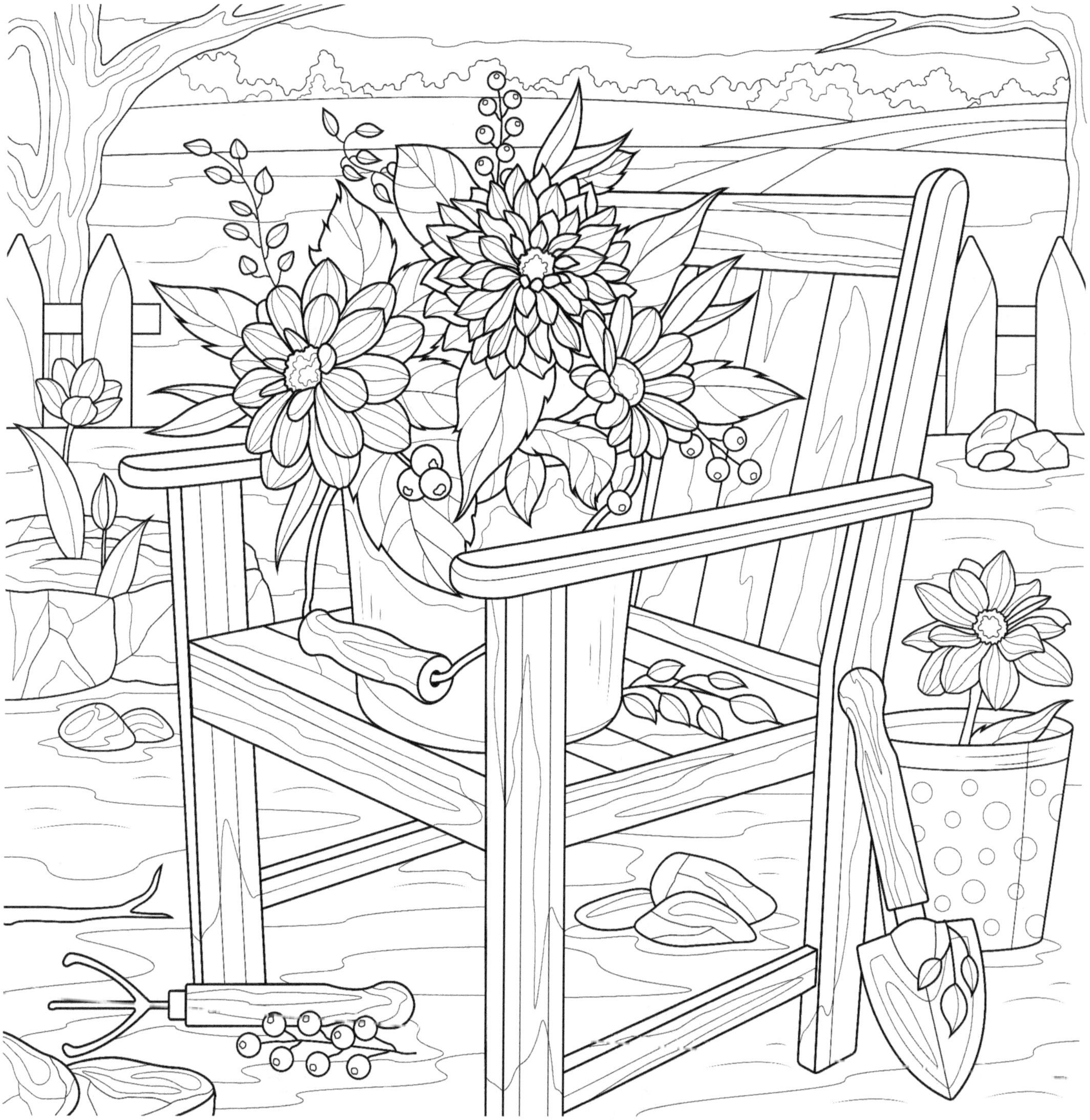

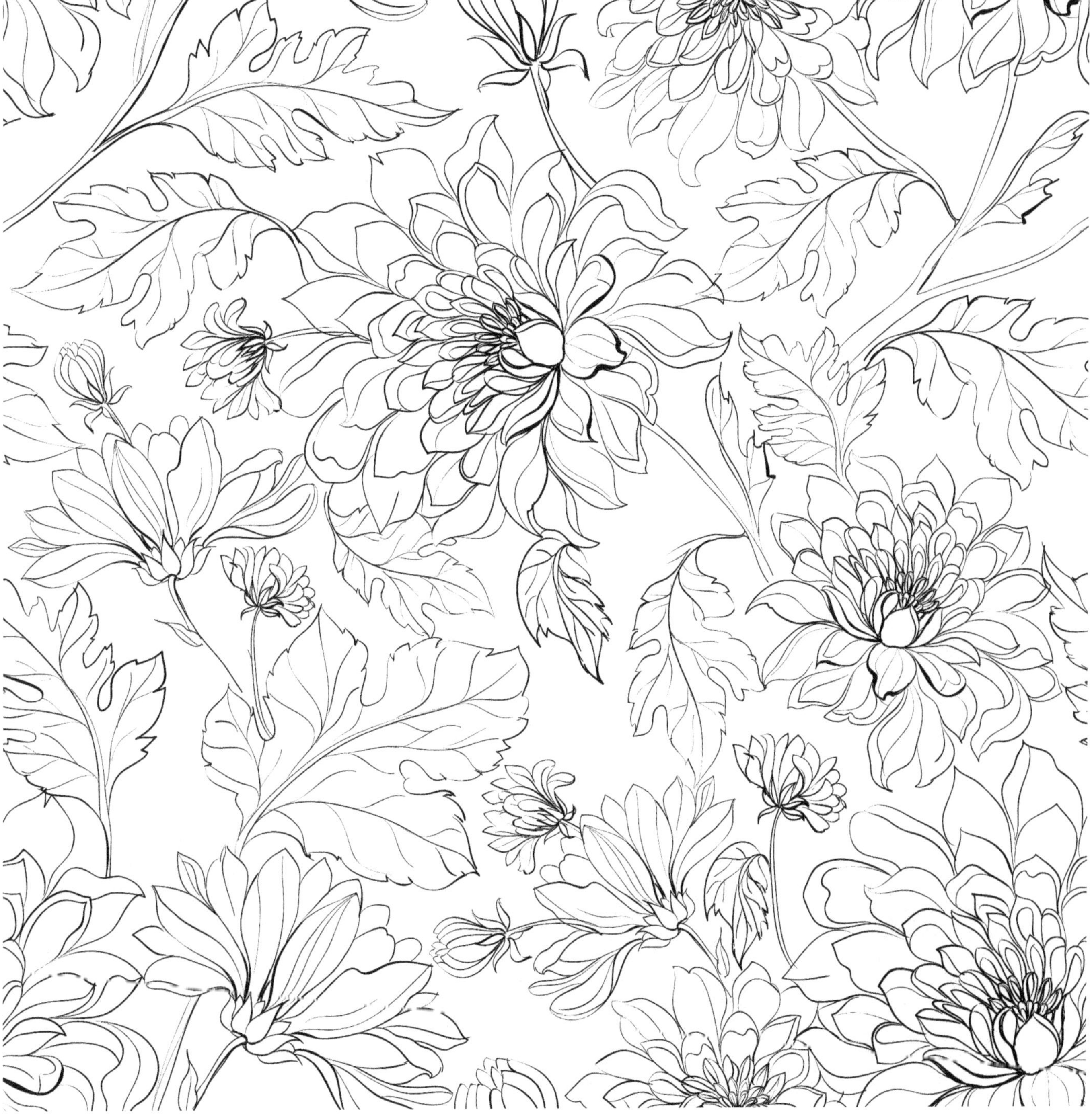

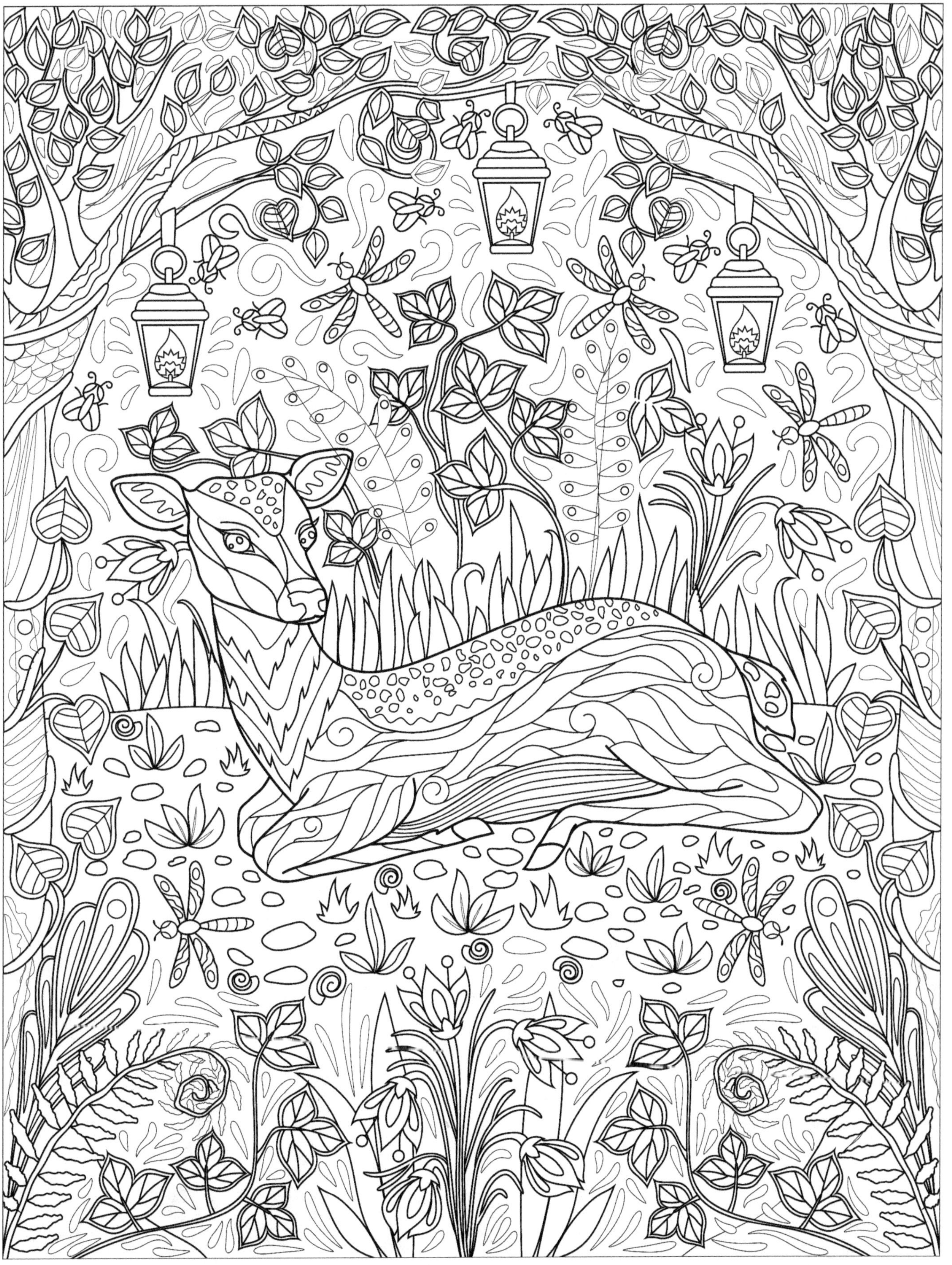

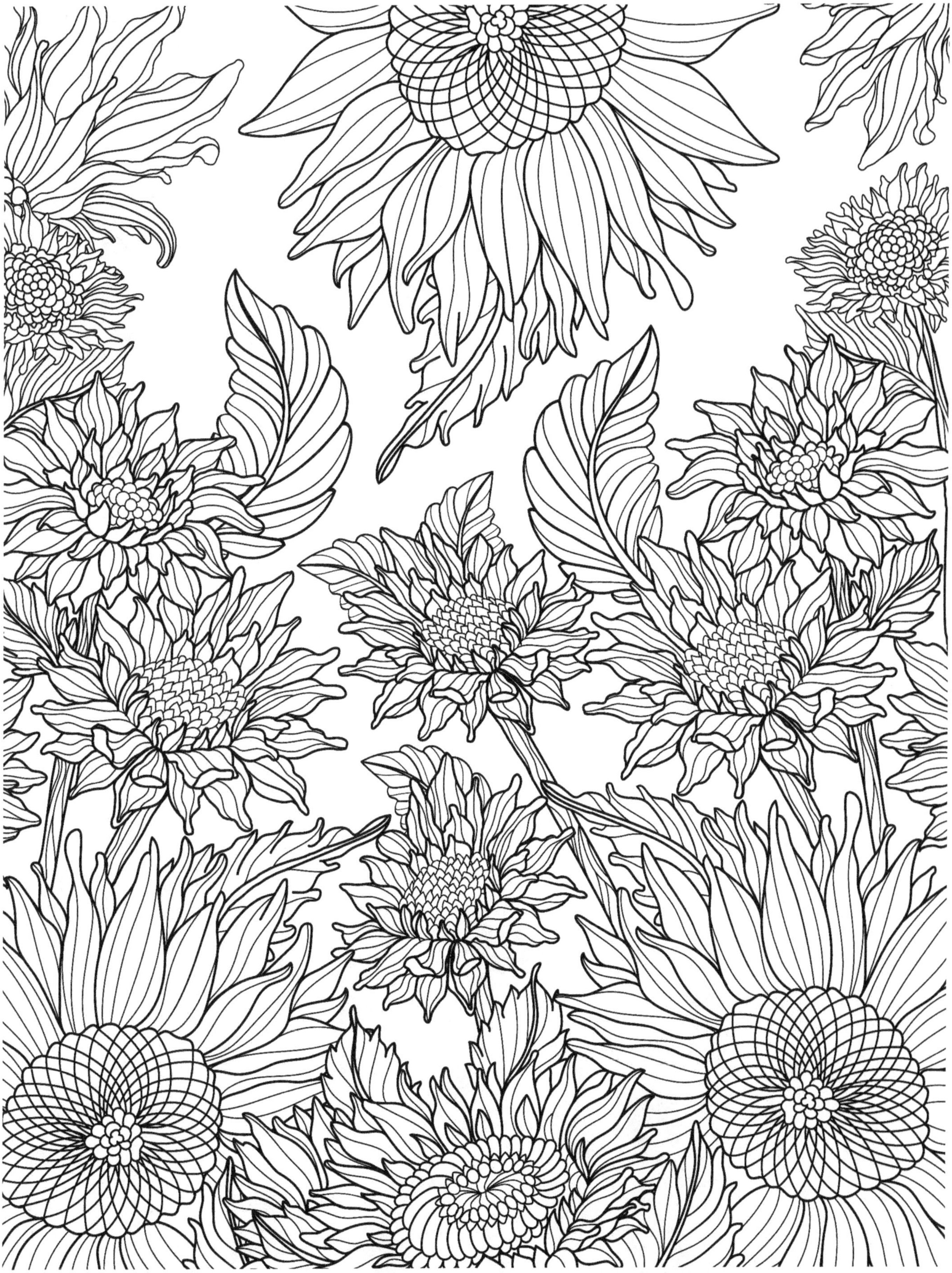

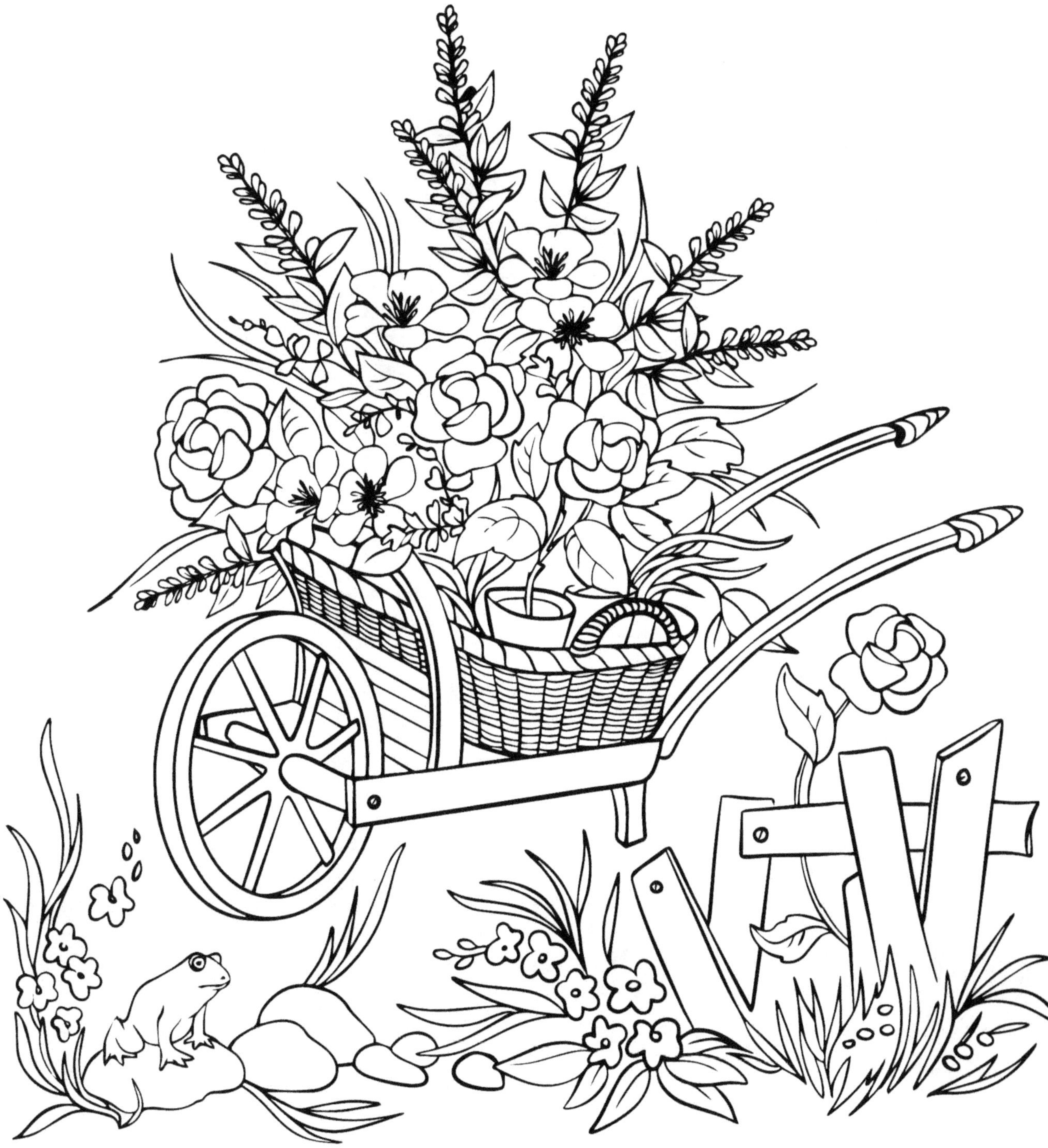

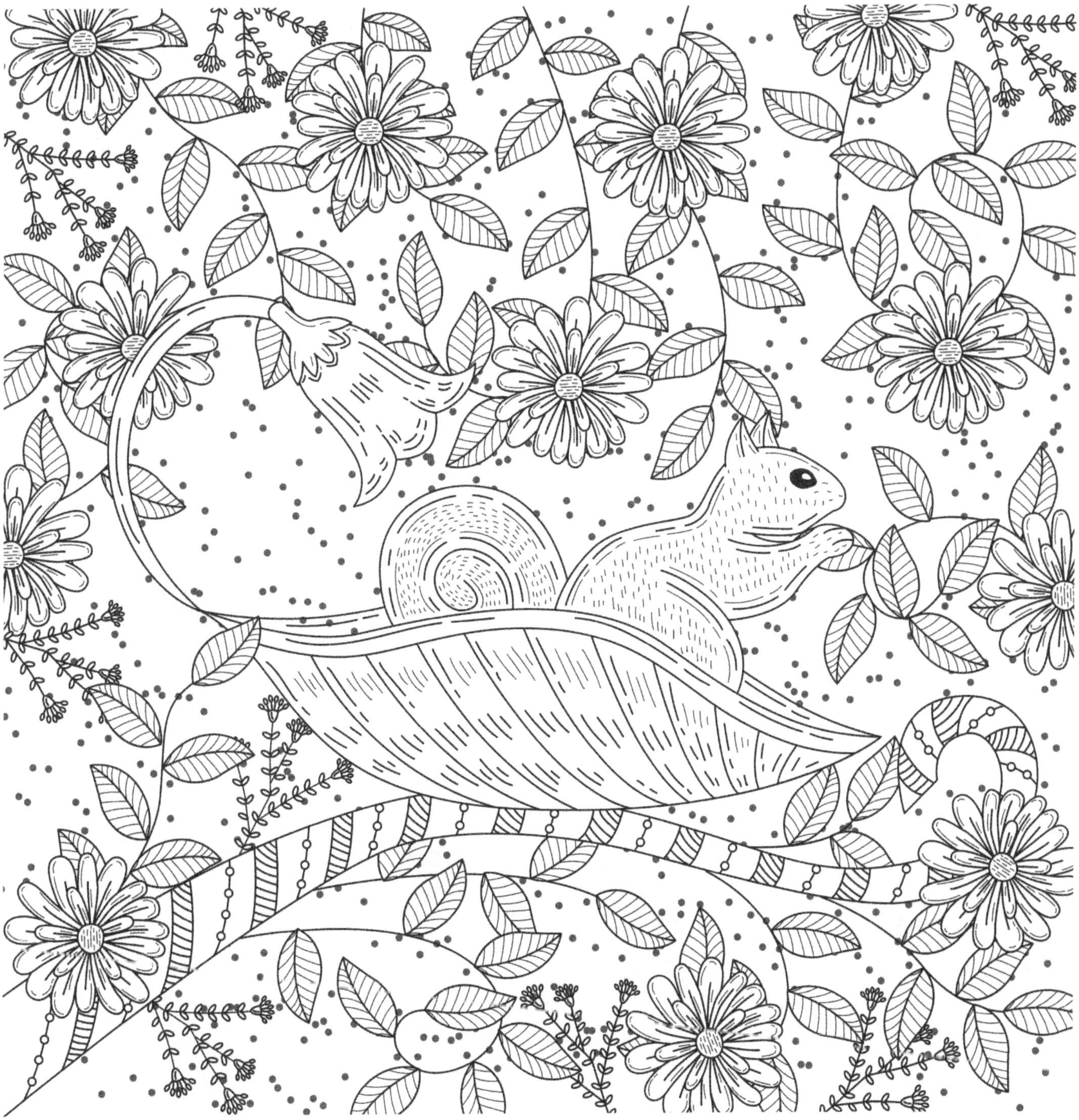

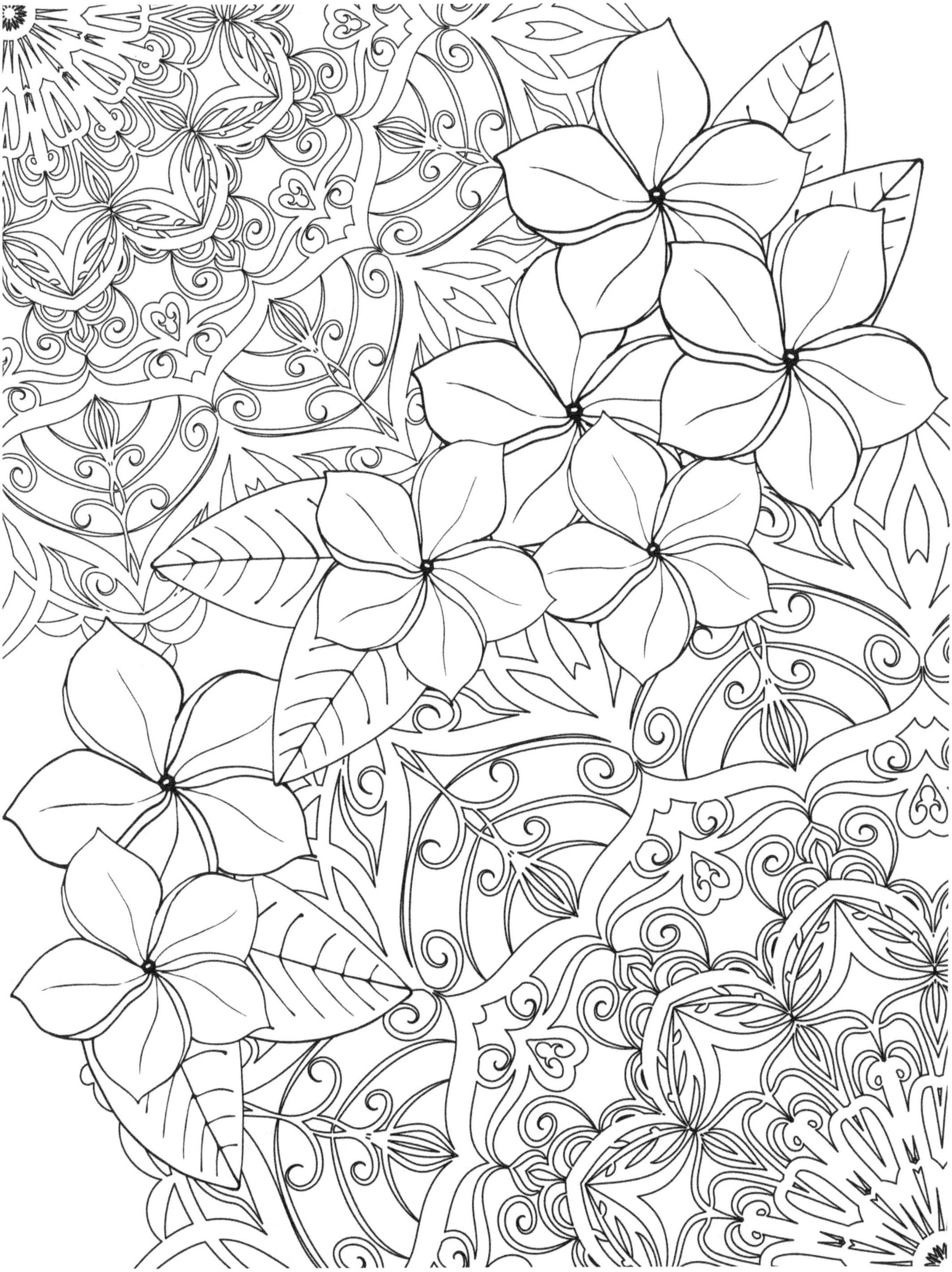

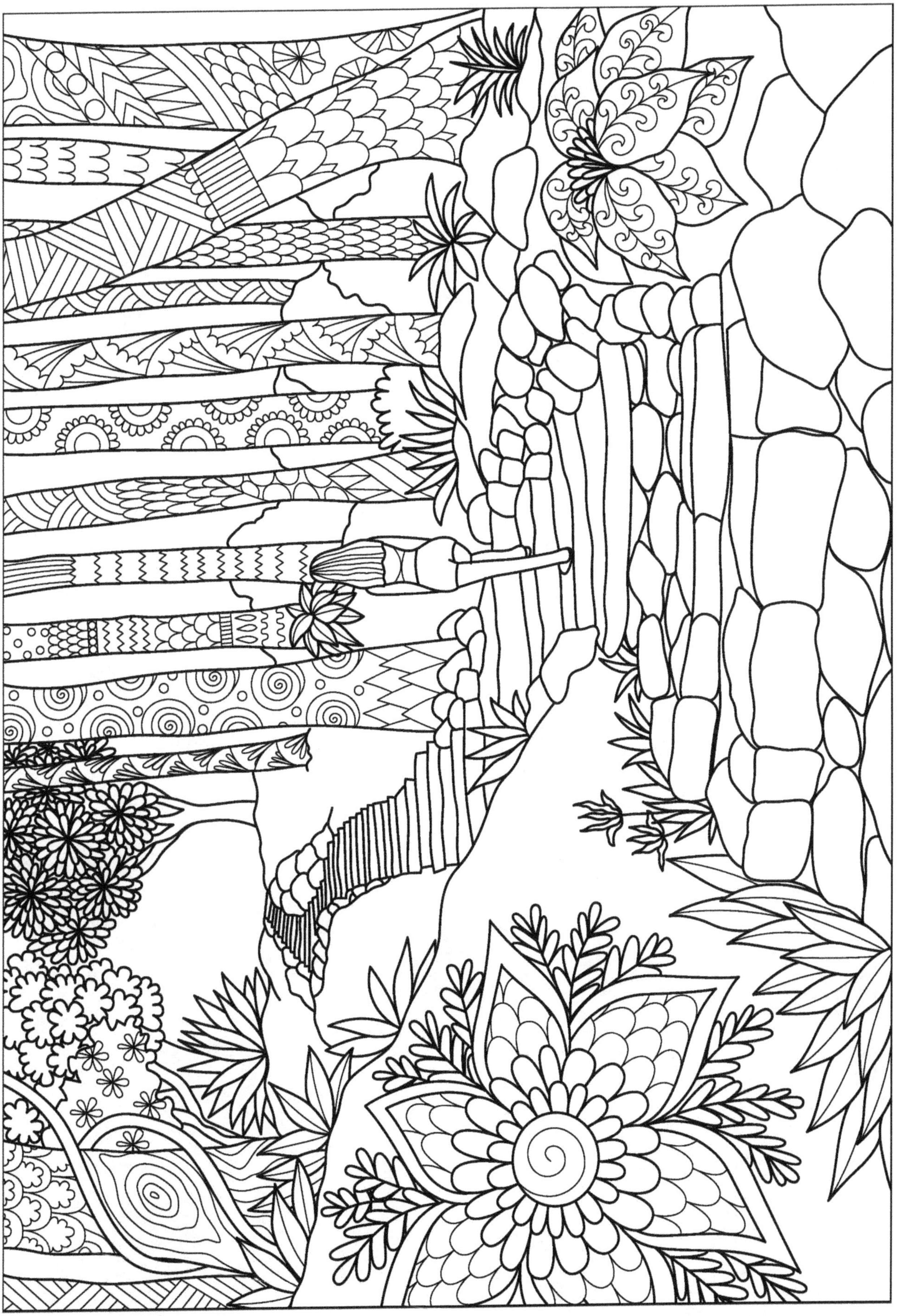

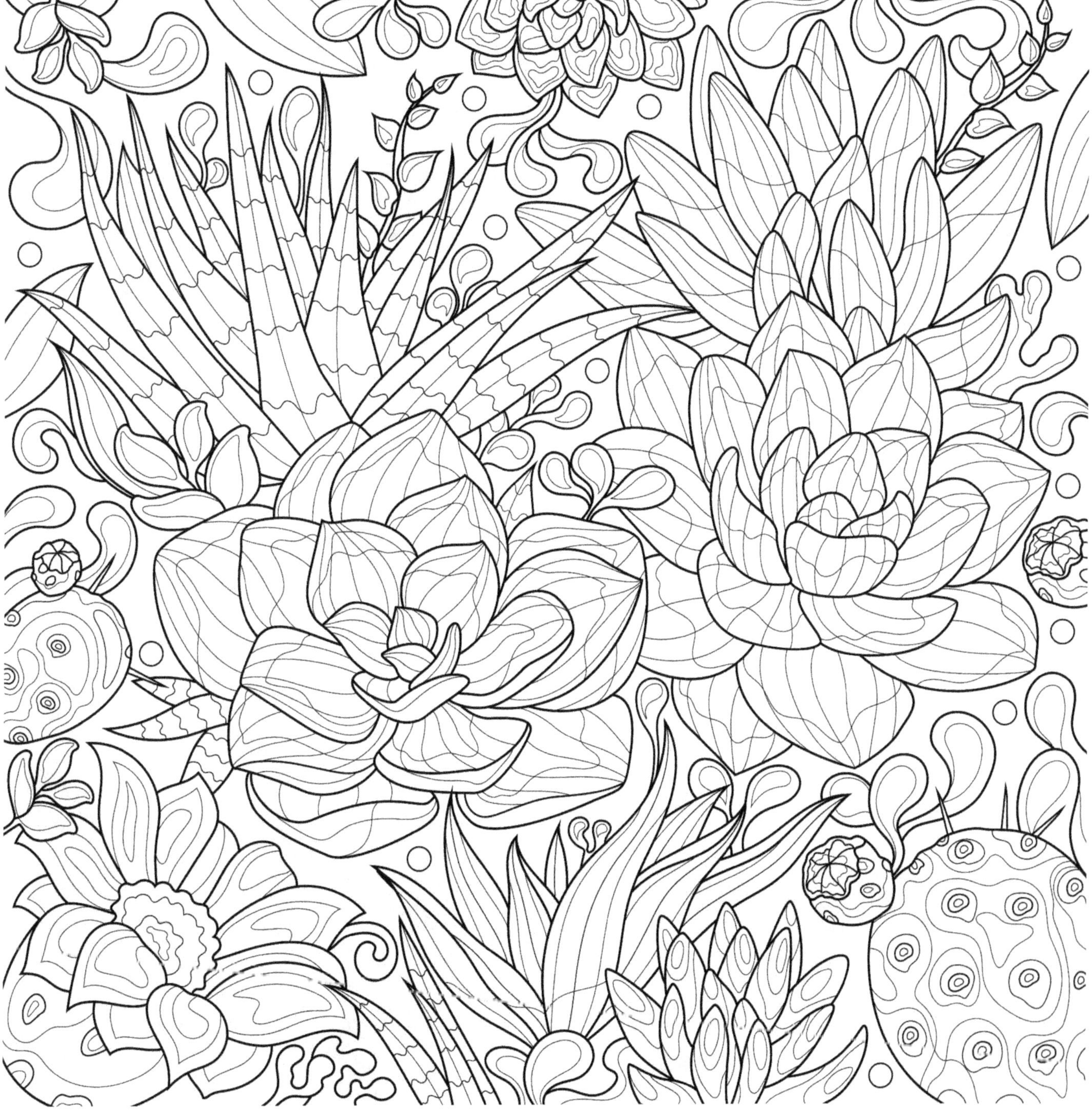

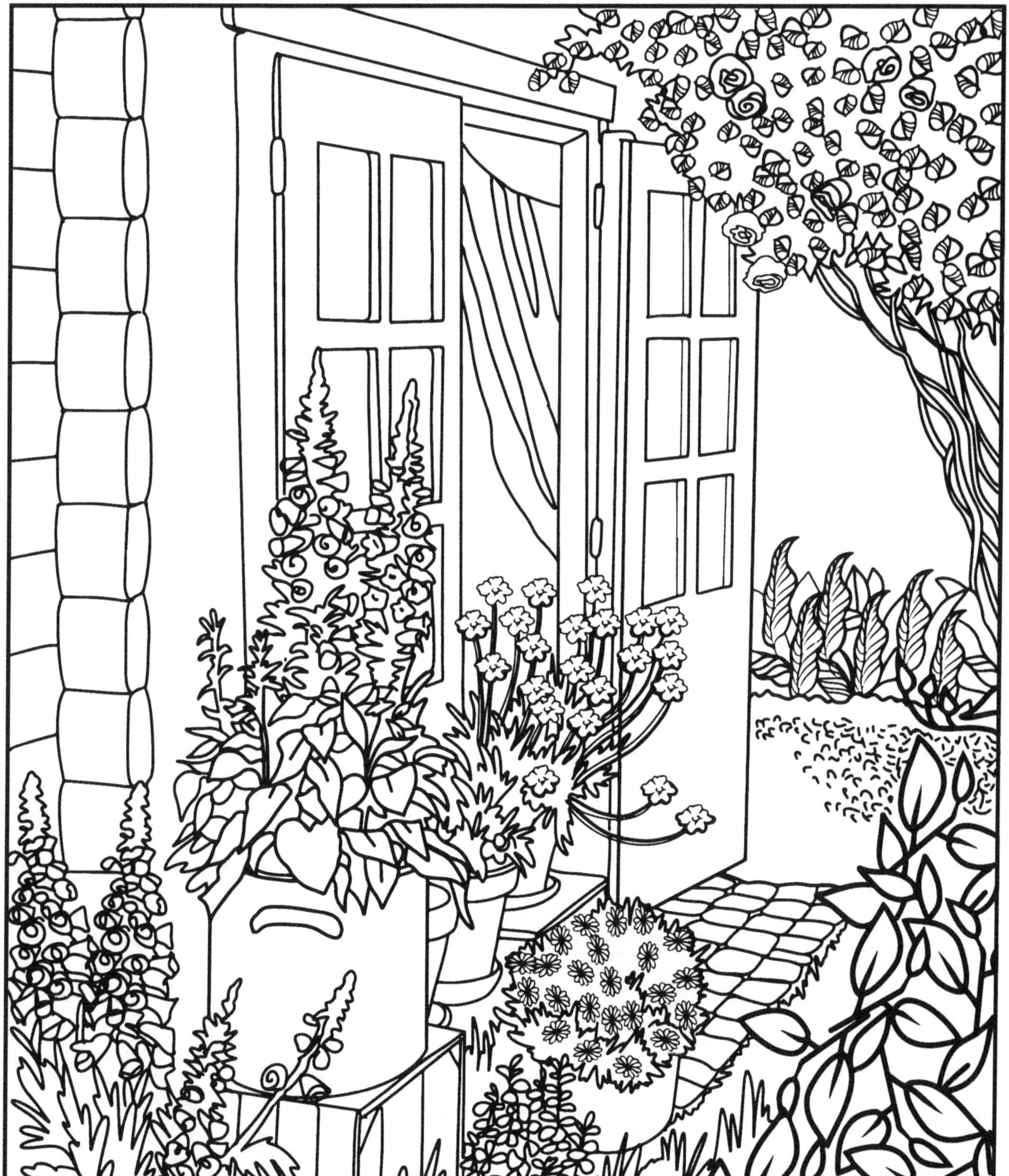

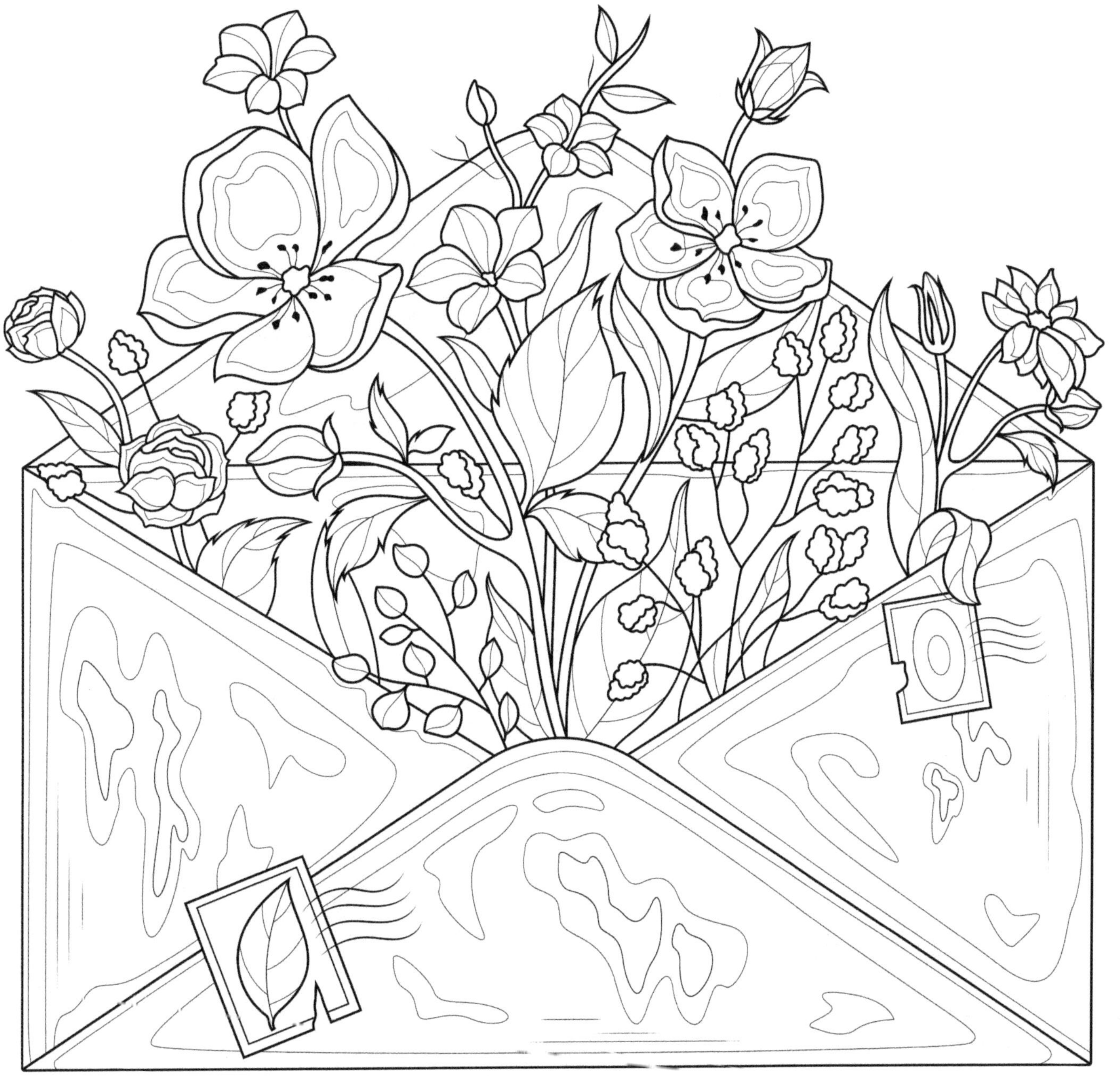

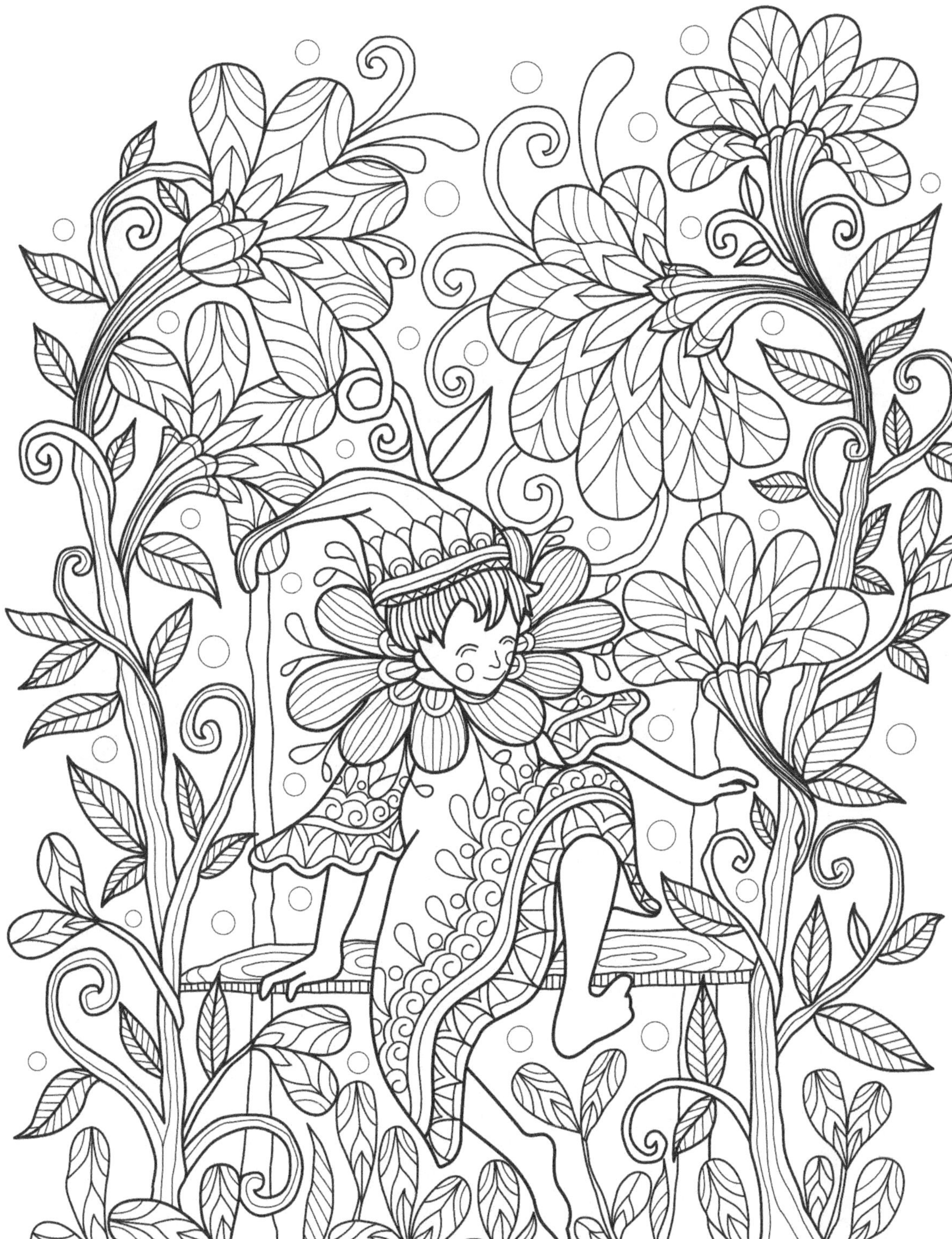

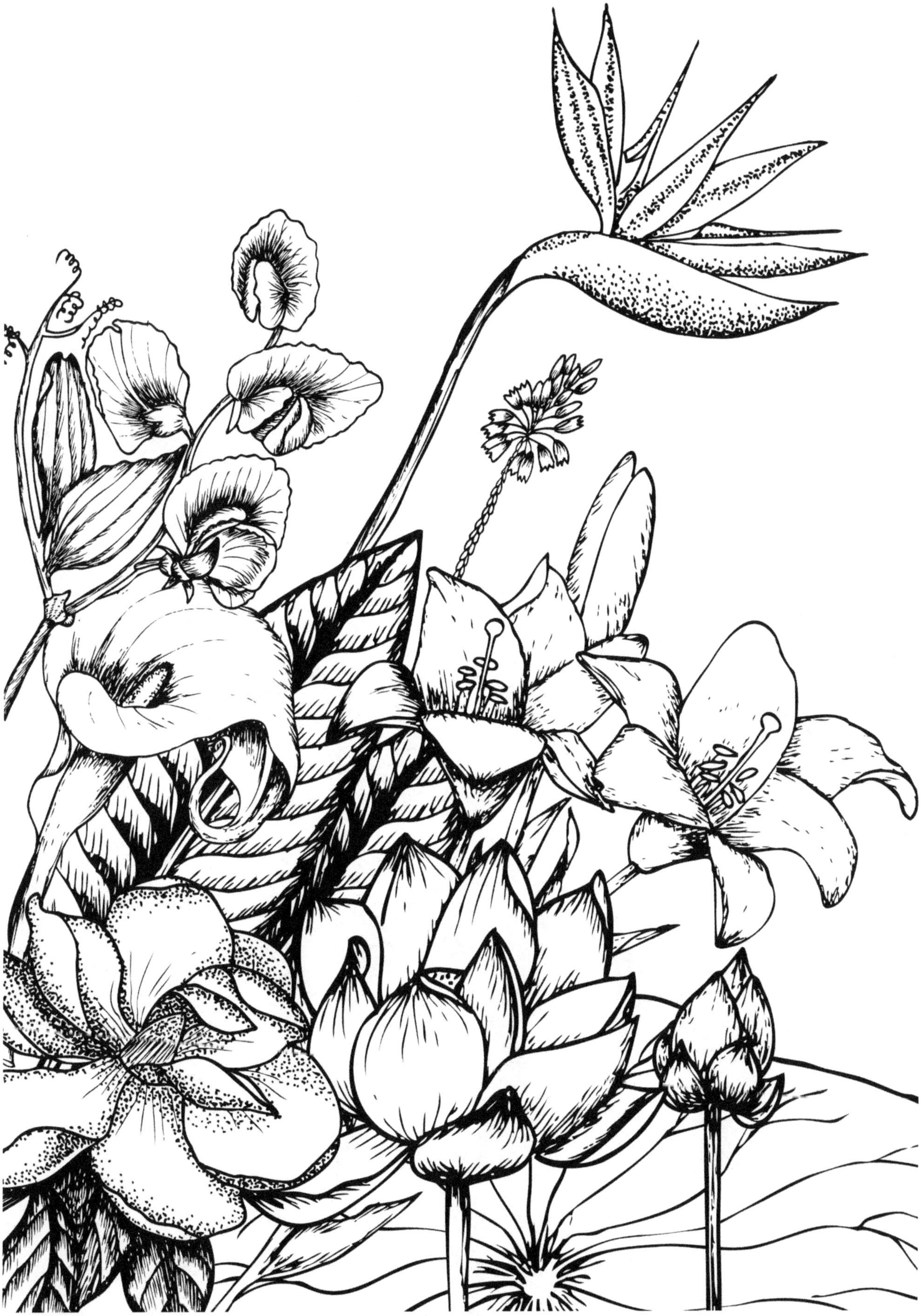

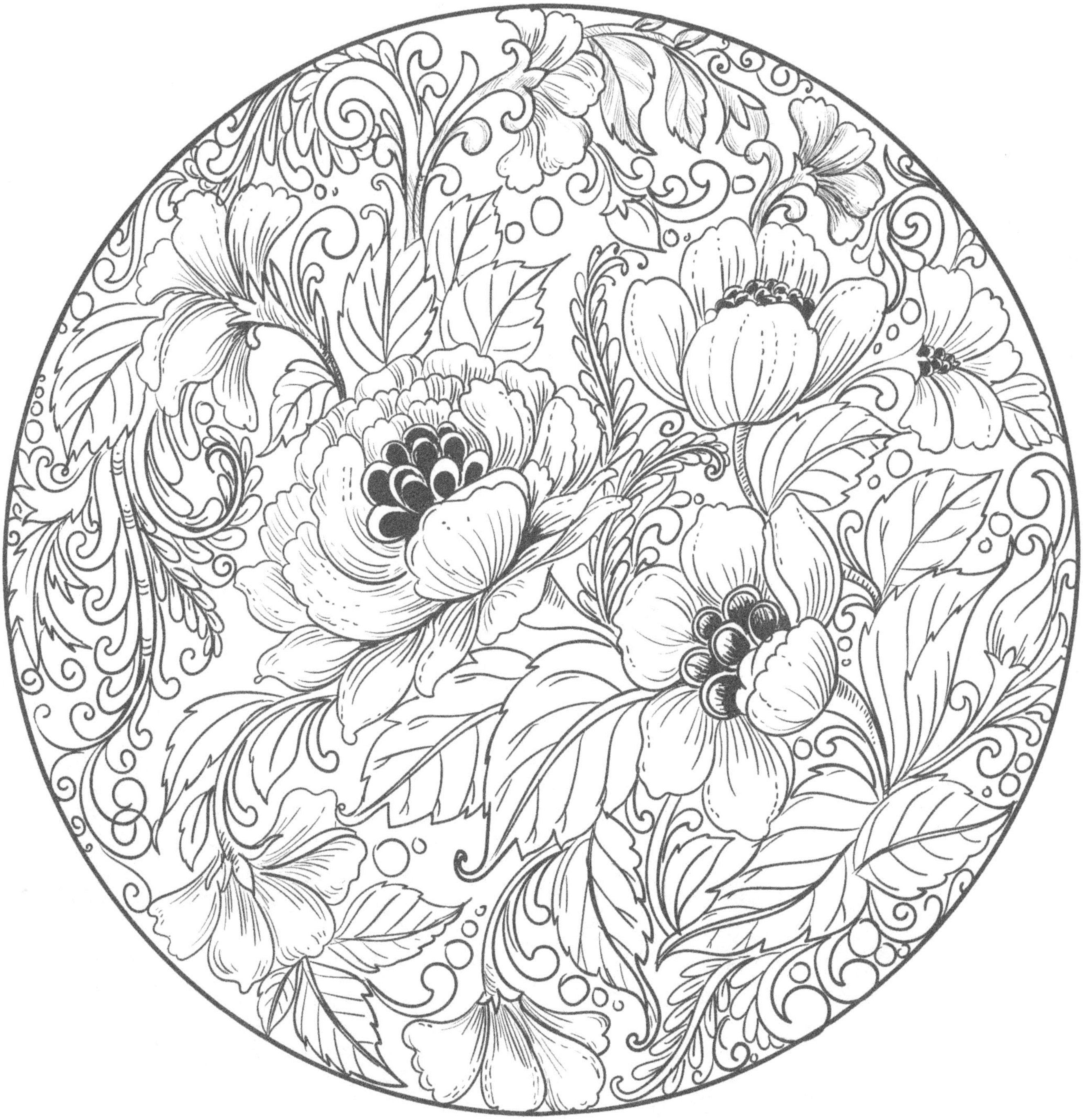

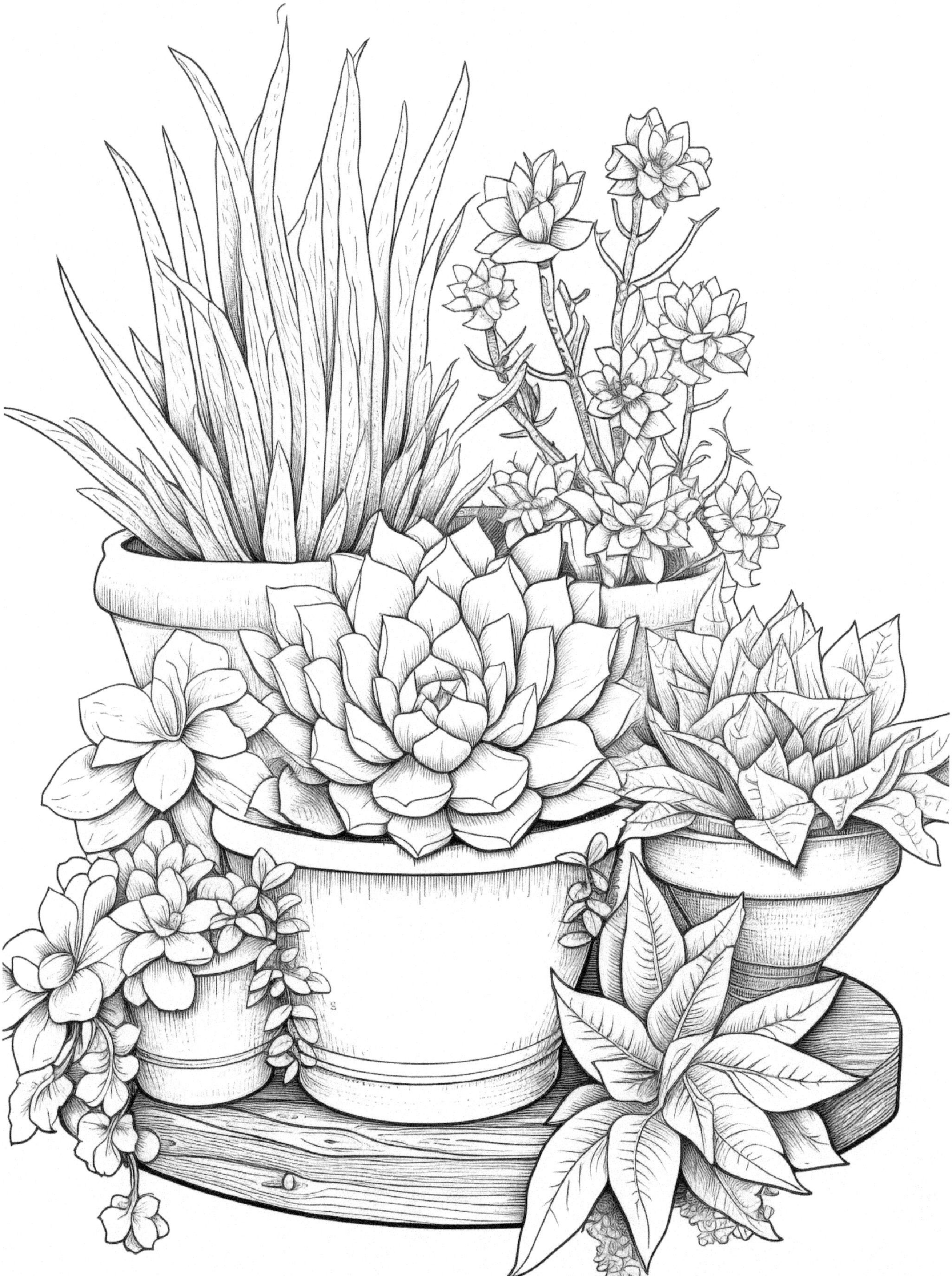

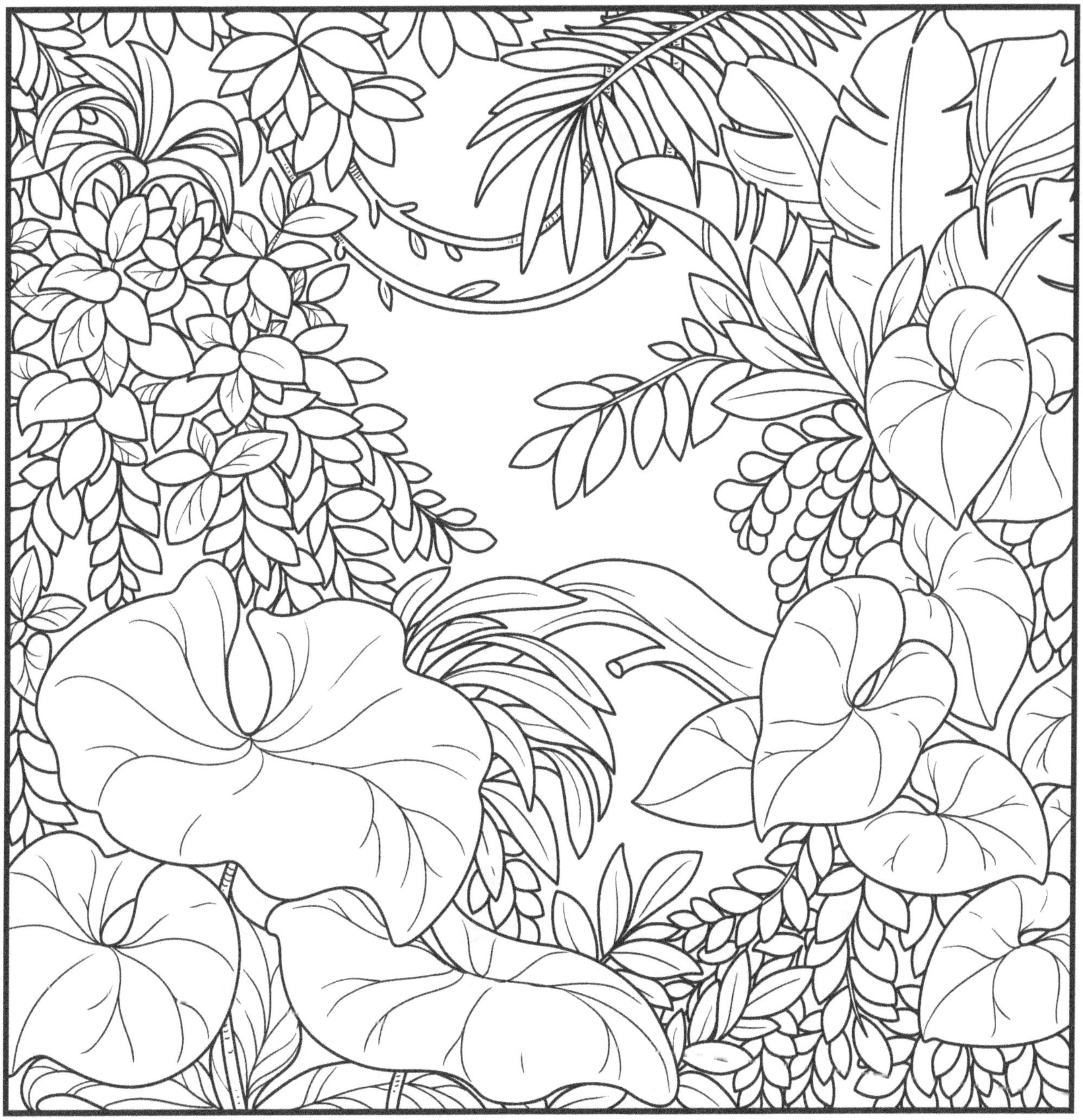

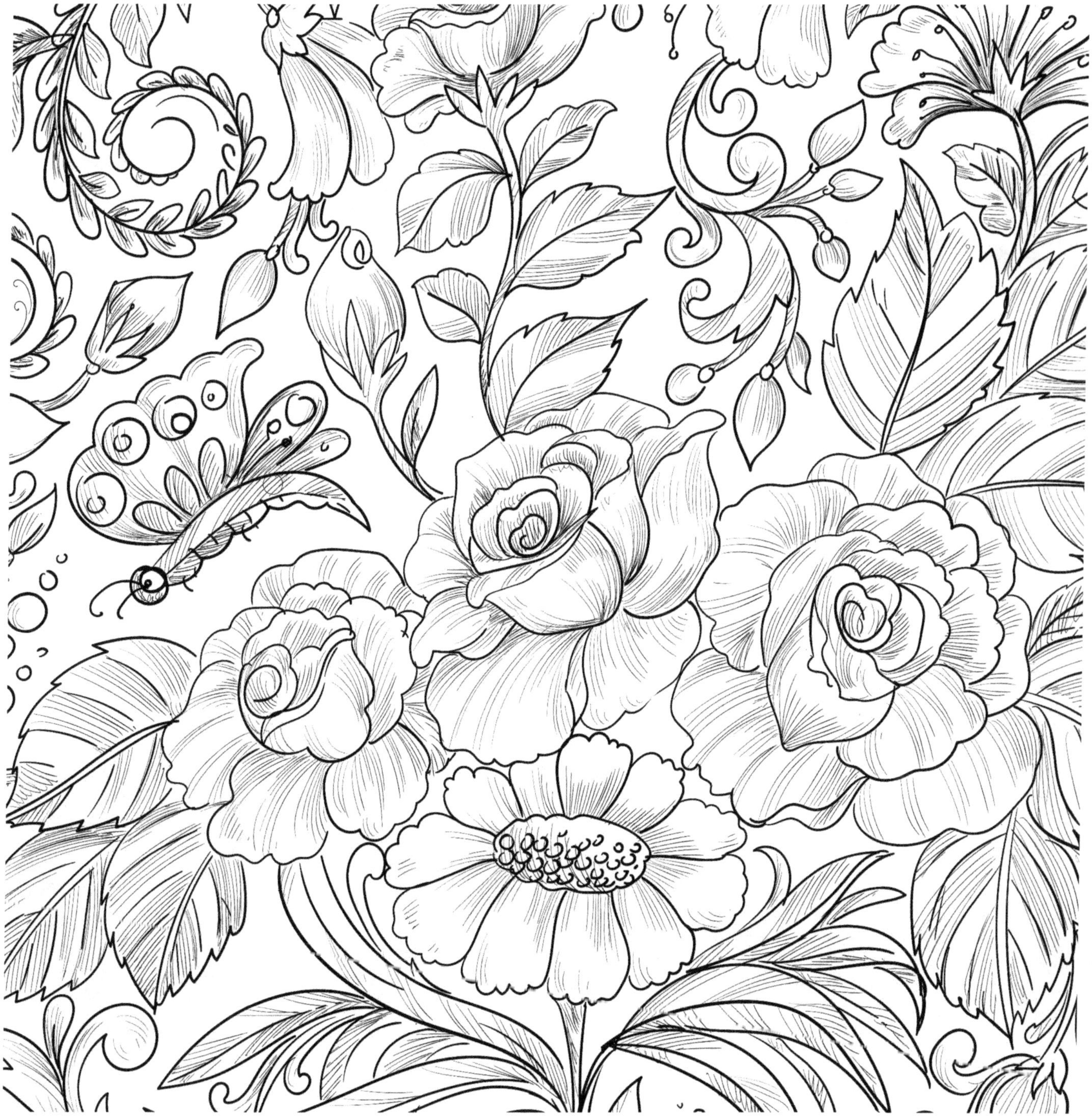

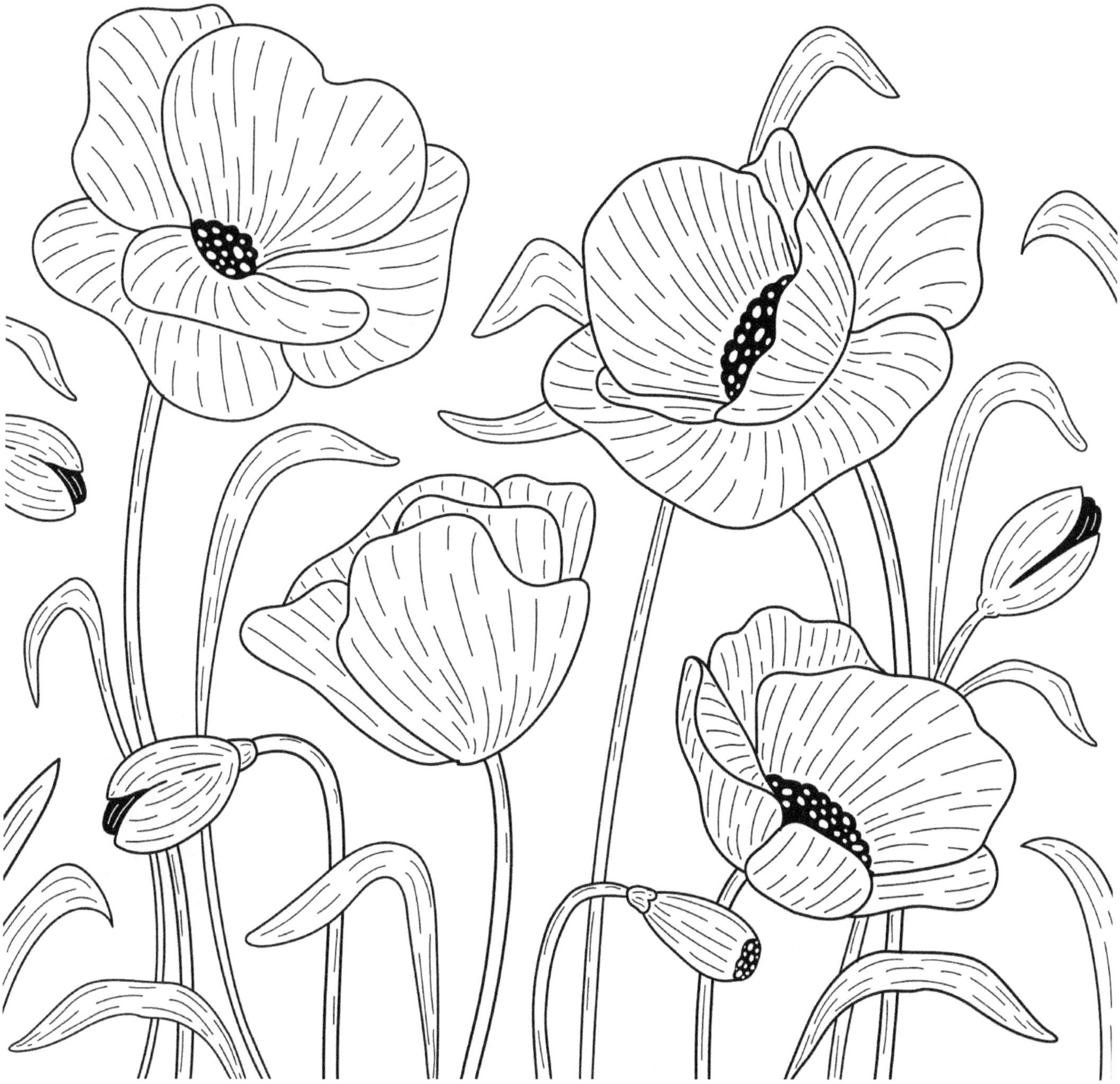

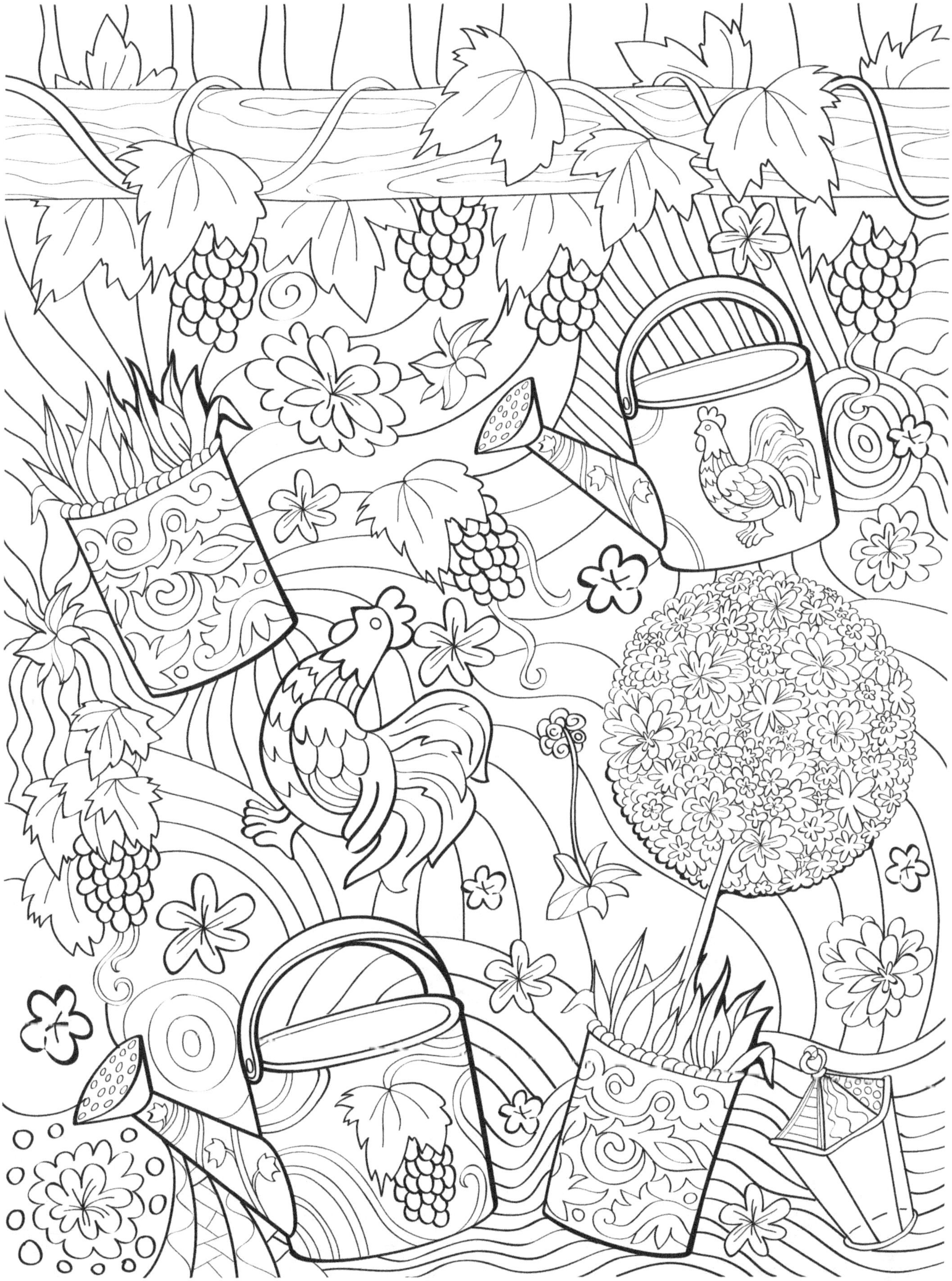

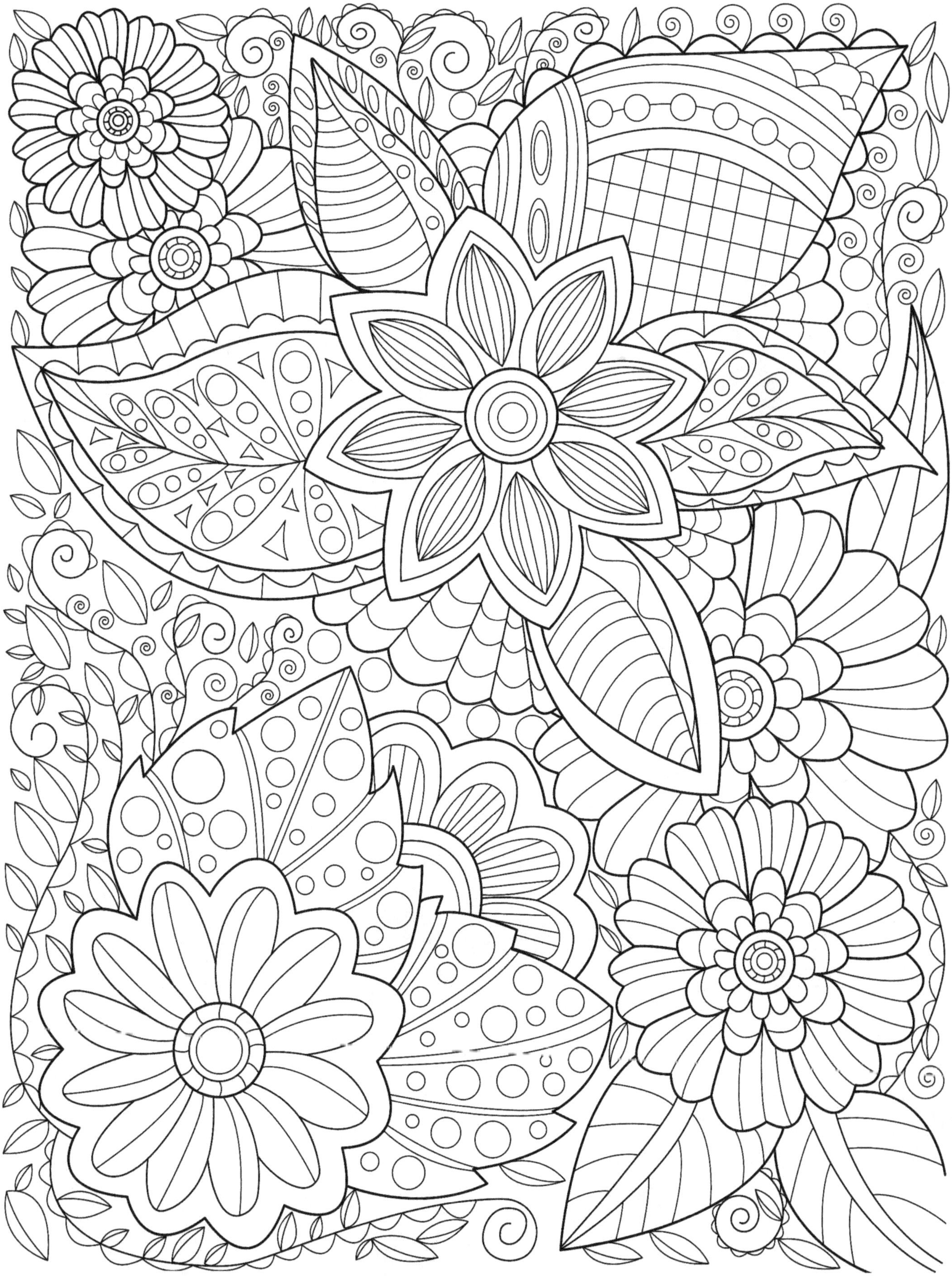

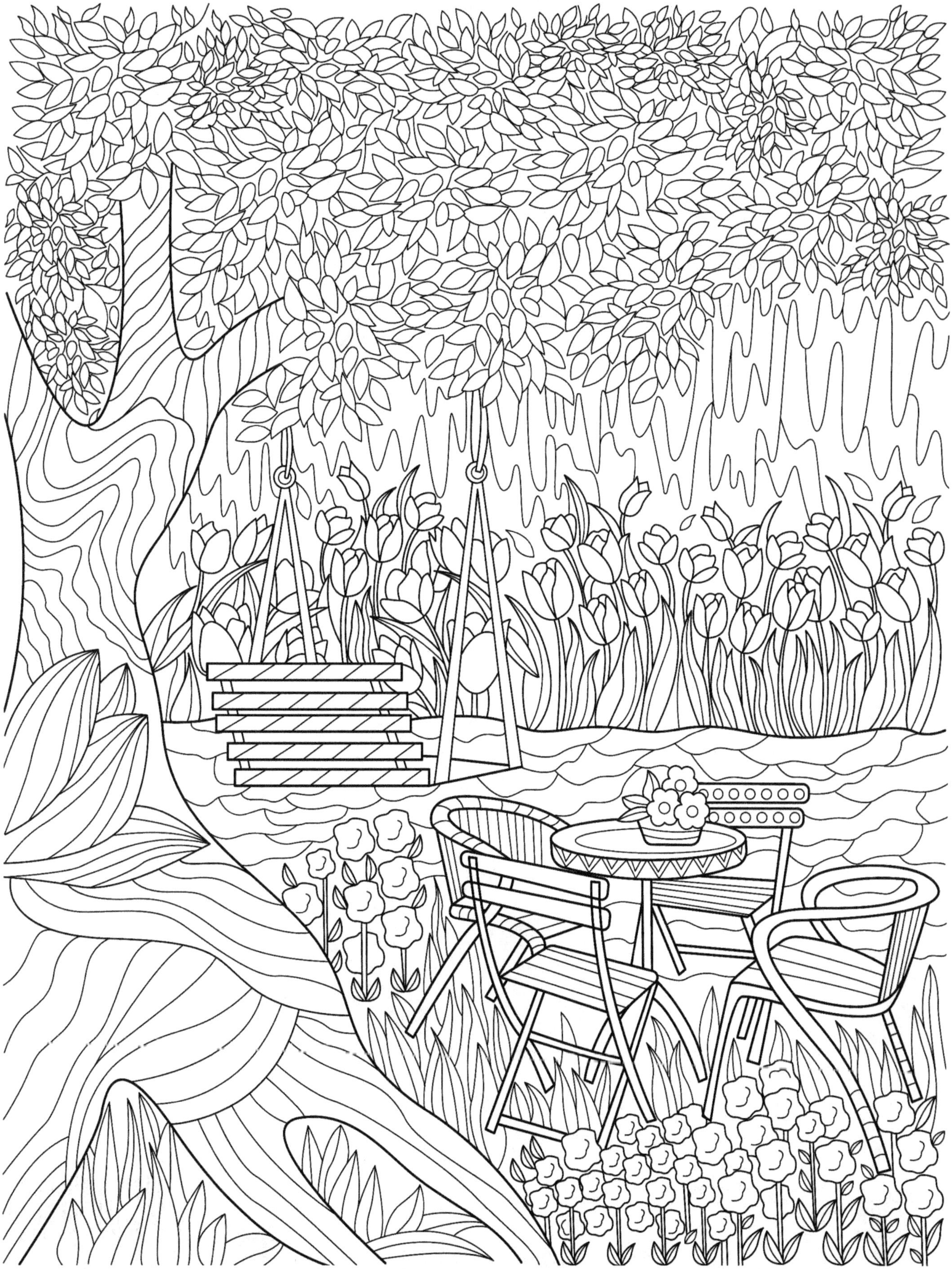

CPSIA information can be obtained
at www.ICGtesting.com
Printed in the USA
BVHW021935080623
665636BV00011B/574

9 798211 190931